D0237211

WOMAN'S OWN
BOOK OF
FLOWER ARRANGEMENTS

Healthy Planet
Books for Free
You've rescued me from going to waste

healthyplanet.org
healthy_planet   healthyplanet

woman's own BOOK OF flower arrangements

PAUL HAMLYN

LONDON · NEW YORK · SYDNEY · TORONTO

Published by
THE HAMLYN PUBLISHING GROUP LIMITED
LONDON · NEW YORK · SYDNEY · TORONTO
Hamlyn House, Feltham, Middlesex, England

© Copyright The Hamlyn Publishing Group Limited 1966, 1967
Third Impression 1969

SBN 600 40339 4

Printed in Italy by Arnoldo Mondadori – Officine Grafiche – Verona

CONTENTS

The Editor is grateful to the British flower industry, through the Flowers and Plants Council, for providing many colour photographs and other help. She also thanks the Bulb Information Desk for their help

COLOUR ILLUSTRATIONS

FLOWER ARRANGING MADE EASY

Anyone can be an artist with flowers. Anyone, that is, who is not afraid to experiment and let imagination run riot. The first thing to realise is that *you* can do it. This is the one form of art that anyone can learn and enjoy right from the very first attempt.

The pictures that you create will reflect your own personality and individuality; no-one else will produce exactly the same design as you, even with identical materials. Agree? Then the time to begin is now. Start using flowers to make pictures that appeal to your own eye for beauty.

In the art of flower arranging there is no mystery, there are no hard and fast rules and regulations. Do not let yourself become blinded by science. You will not have to spend pounds on specialised equipment. There is such infinite scope in flower arranging that you can afford to give yourself a free hand. But as in every other form of art there are a few basic principles to remember – and there are a number of short cuts already found by the experts.

This *expertese*, culled from many sources, can help you towards success more quickly than if you were to rely on your own unaided efforts; and it will stimulate your artistic imagination in the early days. After a while, the marvellous results and the compliments of your friends will be the only stimulus needed to stir you to more and better things.

This, then, is the purpose of the *Woman's Own Book of Flower Arrangements*. Firstly, to introduce you to the art of arranging flowers. More and more women everywhere are turning to flower arranging as a form of self-expression which also gives pleasure to others. Secondly, it is to show you how to begin; to give you the basic knowledge necessary for your very first arrangement. And finally, it is to give you the spur to go on by showing you photographs of the glorious displays created by others, both professional and amateur flower arrangers.

On the following pages you will find simple but detailed information on every aspect of flower arranging; the different styles are described and the basic principles of design and composition explained. We discuss fully the pros and cons of the various types of equipment and containers available; and tell you how to get the utmost in beauty out of every one of your precious blooms.

If you have a garden you'll discover the best flowers and foliage to grow for effect – even the humble carrot and beetroot have valuable foliage to contribute. If all flowers must be bought, we suggest how to make the most of a few. We take you through the seasons of the year with their special problems and special delights. And we show you how to design arrangements for particular locations in your home and elsewhere.

Our chapter on arranging Church flowers will be of special interest to all those who help in their parish by regularly or occasionally "doing" the flowers in church. This chapter was written by Mrs. Molly Purefoy, whose lovely displays in Tewkesbury Abbey have given pleasure to so many visitors.

A chapter which will, we feel, be of particular interest, is the one dealing with arrangements for Shows. The membership of the numerous Flower Clubs and Flower Arrangement sections of local Horticultural Societies is growing year by year and many readers will welcome advice on this aspect of arranging.

We feel that there is one especial section that you will turn to again and again. We have called it "How to make cut flowers last" – know-how you might discover for yourself in time and with luck – but here in black and white for you to note and benefit from straight away.

For example, how would you coax a spray of spring buds into blossom? Do you know how such common-or-garden commodities as sugar and charcoal can be used to make your arrangements more effective? The answers to these questions are included in chapter twelve, together with other useful information.

As we said in the beginning there are no hard and fast rules to the art of flower arranging. There are, however, five common-sense tips:

1. Simplicity is the secret of good flower arrangements; so let simplicity be your guide.
2. Stems of equal length deprive you of scope in your flower arrangements, so cut your flower stems to different lengths.
3. Give every flower a chance to look its best. This means "breathing space" for every flower with no flower hiding another. When arranging buds, do allow enough room for their expansion into full bloom.
4. If in difficulty, try using the basic shape of a triangle: place three flowers in key positions and go on from there.
5. Floral colours don't clash so you can mix colours as much as you like. Massing flowers in blocks of colours is, however, more effective than scattering different colours throughout an arrangement.

When buying flowers, and especially spring flowers grown from bulbs, one thing to be kept in mind is the advantage of buying in bud. The full bloom of a flower is a delight to behold. But there is as much beauty and more enjoyment in watching a bud develop from its first tinges of colour to glorious full bloom as there is in the bloom itself.

In the spring, take a bunch of tulips in bud, or a bunch of daffodils, narcissi or irises in bud, and arrange them, or a mixture of them, in a vase giving each one adequate breathing space and room to expand.

You now have a picture which will change subtly for you as the days go by. Each time you glance at it there will be fresh enjoyment.

Fresh enjoyment, too, can be found on your country walks as your interest in flower arranging grows. Our countryside — English, Irish, Scottish, Welsh — in all its incomparable variety offers untold delight for the flower-lover. Every month of the year shows a different aspect of the wonderful face of nature.

Rich inspiration for new arrangements comes from the sight of growing flowers, grasses, berries and trees. Even the most ordinary weed, one so familiar that you may previously never have looked at it, can have a part to play in a "wild" arrangement.

With an eye on future design, cultivate the habit of examining almost everything that grows. Consider carefully whether this branch would blend well with that flower or with those grasses; or even with the shells you brought back from last year's summer holiday.

In our lush woodlands you may find unusual small plants growing under larger plants or trees, withered branches or pieces of bark. You may see a branch growing in exactly the right curve for a particular design you have been planning and with care you might be able to remove it. There are so many possible finds, some of great beauty, and it is incredibly satisfying to place these unusual discoveries in your own special settings.

In wilder country search for stones of an interesting shape or in an attractive colour — these too will find a place in your flower displays. The more you train your eyes to see exciting possibilities, the more original your arrangements.

This spring arrangement of tulips and apple blossom is held in the goblet container by crumpled chicken wire. It is wise to buy tulips in bud, then you can watch them unfold

Wild flowers can be exquisite in their delicacy, breath-taking in their colour and range, and there can be nothing to equal the joy of suddenly coming on a woody glade filled with bluebells; or a grassy bank in May yellow with cowslips.

People who love flowers would never harm them by snatching them indiscriminately and wastefully; a small bunch picked with care is all that is necessary.

Bracken, dock and cow parsley (known to country people in some parts by the prettier name of Queen Anne's lace), sprays of elder or rowan, stalks of golden barley or wheat — all these can add grace and favour to your designs.

If before starting your walk you equip yourself with a polythene bag and some damp cotton wool to wrap round the stems, then so much the better.

Most wild material is inclined to wilt fairly quickly but if steeped in deep, cold water for some hours it will revive and harden. Large surfaced leaves should be placed flat in water for a while. This treatment will help them to hold their shape without flagging.

The countryside is a marvellous source of supply for foliage, leaves and grasses for your store cupboard. Each autumn it is worth making several trips in order to replenish for the winter. During the first week of September place branches of beech leaves in a jug containing one part glycerine to two parts water and leave them there for three weeks. This will preserve them and keep them shiny for the rest of the winter.

Other leaves can also be preserved in this way — it is fun to experiment with different finds and to note their differing reactions. Fern leaves dry well if placed between sheets of newspaper and left for some weeks under a mattress or an unused carpet. Seed pods, dried grasses and reeds look starkly beautiful in winter arrangements.

Berries, too, are bright and delightful accessories to autumn and winter arrangements but after

A few roses imaginatively displayed in an Italian wine bottle — the effect is casual but it was very carefully planned. Note the large flower low in the arrangement

This classic triangular display of dahlia blooms and buds in a goblet is held firmly in wire netting. The smaller, darker flowers around the outside and the large flowers in the centre give movement to the design

a while in a dry atmosphere they begin to fall; buy some clear shellac or varnish from the ironmongers or household stores to preserve them and give them a wonderfully shiny appearance.

Gourds grown in the garden, lovely rich-looking horse-chestnuts (perhaps a few of the children's conkers whisked away from under their noses), acorns and oak-apples, all of these may be varnished and used in your arrangements.

If you have large areas to cover with varnish, and if you are impatient, take a short cut: mix some builders' size and when it is cool dip a whole branch or cluster into the mixture, afterwards hanging it up to drain and dry.

These are just a few ideas which are to be gleaned from a country walk, a few ways with varied materials that are yours for the finding.

Turning again to cultivated flowers, it occasionally happens that someone who can design a delightful arrangement of mixed blooms is at a loss for inspiration when faced with, say, six rosebuds, or a few carnations, or a florist's dozen of any one particular flower. In chapter nine this problem — which is really no problem at all — is discussed in detail. Photographs show numerous displays using one kind of flower only, with and without the addition of foliage, and they are sure to provide you with ideas.

Another point that really does make a world of difference to a design is that larger flowers

look more effective in the centre of a display while smaller flowers look better when placed to the outside. Naturally it is not possible to follow this principle when faced with a bunch of identical blooms but it is useful when selecting from the garden or the florists' shop.

The two following chapters cover the two main styles of flower arranging: Mass (formal or classical) Style; and Line Design.

The Mass Style has long been widely practised in this country and most beginners master the basic principles of this style first; but Line Design is today becoming increasingly popular. In great part this is due to the influence of the westernised version of the Japanese style of flower arranging which has great charm and beauty.

The big difference between the two main styles is that Mass Style creates its dramatic effect from its many flowers and contrasting shapes, colours and textures; whereas Line Design depends for its appeal on the shape of its basic outline and the quality of each flower, branch or piece of foliage.

As you progress with your designs you may discover a decided preference or aptitude for one or the other; or you may find that you become equally adept with both styles.

In the art of flower arranging, as in every other art, there are certain words which have particular

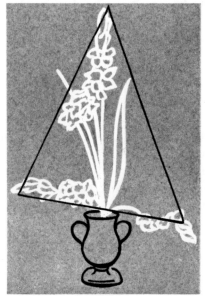

STEP-BY-STEP GUIDE TO BASIC TRIANGULAR DESIGN

Fill container with crumpled wire mesh, or special cellular plastic substance. Place longest central stem in position to form the peak of the triangle and see that it is firmly in place

Choose from among your flowers two long, light yet firm stems, place them to left and right to form the base corners. The angles will determine the finished shape of your arrangement

Fill in body of the arrangement with flowers, cutting the stems shorter where necessary. Add some foliage and water then arrange more blooms to soften the edge of the container

Left: these flowers were especially arranged as a display for the month of March. The tulips, which should be bought in bud for longer life, were cut to varying lengths and arranged in a tall conical vase.

meanings, names for the various tools of the trade which you will use and which will quickly become familiar. More about them later but there are a few words which you need to know at once. *Material*: this rather ordinary-sounding word conjures up pictures of delight to flower arrangers; it means blooms and buds, branches and twigs, grasses, leaves and foliage, pretty stones and coloured shells — anything, in fact, which is capable of being beautifully arranged. *Containers* describes anything in or on which a flower display is arranged; vases, of course, but also trinket boxes, copper pots, soup tureens, cake tins, jelly moulds — anything suitable from

around the house which comes to mind. *Holders* includes all the various articles which actually hold the flowers firmly in the container. And "firmly" is the operative word. Chicken wire, pin holders, packs of light, cellular material are those most often used.

The would-be flower arranger should equip herself with a suitable container, a pin holder or some wire netting or (best) both, a pair of scissors and she is ready to begin.

Anyone who has ever placed a few flowers with care into a vase and standing back to admire felt a glow of pleasure is already more than half-way there!

MASS STYLE

The general interpretation of the term "a mass or formal arrangement" is a full vase of flowers — beautiful flowers arranged in some profusion in a lovely vase. The mass arrangement demands a conventional design and one which will fit into a conventional background. It is not a stark design based on a single line or curve.

In line designs it is an idea or a mood which is portrayed, but the formal massed style shows off the beauty and colouring of the flowers. It is a style that is traditionally British, and is ideal for so many of our lovely garden flowers. Blooms such as sweet peas, roses, lilies, orchids, delphiniums and the more choice flowers are considered suitable for these formal arrangements. Colour is also relevant. Mauve, purple, pink, crimson and blue, as well as subtle colours, are suitable.

Start your actual arrangement by placing a little water in your vase (you top it up when the design is finished) and then put in some crumpled netting. This is usually known as "chicken wire", and it should not be of too small a mesh. The two-inch wire is best for general use as it enables the flowers to be placed at almost any angle. (A small mesh is only advisable for flowers with thin stems.) The secret of success is to cram your container with the crumpled netting, filling it to a trifle above the top of the rim.

As soon as the wire is firmly set, make your outline. If you have planned a triangular outline, place some twigs or tall flowers upright in the centre of the netting first. Then set similar material horizontally on each side to form the base of a triangle. Never be afraid to place your flowers horizontally — the crumpled netting will hold them firmly. One of the most common faults of flower arrangement is to fill a vase with flowers with stalks of the same length and to set them all upright. Although the blooms themselves may be very beautiful, they won't really show to their best advantage and the whole effect is likely to be without personality.

For an asymmetrical massed design, start with the tallest stem, placing off centre at the left, adding large leaves and flowers at the left and longer, finer ones low at the right.

If you are in any doubt about the lines of your design, try to place the flowers to follow the line of the container. In this way you will not go far wrong. For instance, if you are using a large bowl mass your flowers in a big semi-circle.

The Outline Comes First

A good slogan for beginners is, "Never start an arrangement with a round flower." Perhaps there are times when there is nothing else available, but you will be better pleased with the final result if the outline is made with slim sprays, buds or spiky twigs.

Do make sure that the first flowers or twigs are set in the vase as firmly as possible. Whether you start with a tall flower, a branch or some spiky twigs, remember that the rest of your arrangement must be built around it, and so it is vital for it to be fixed very firmly.

Although this first placement can be higher, it should never be less than one and a half times the height of your vase. The width of your design should be two-thirds the height.

After strengthening the outline with a few more flowers, the next important step is to establish a strong point of interest. That is, the place where your eyes will first rest when contemplating the finished arrangement. Do this by placing a large flower, or a group of small ones perhaps of a deeper colour, just over the rim of the vase. You can emphasize this focal point by adding a few leaves, but be careful not to bury these low blooms. Let them be seen.

Stand back now and look at your handiwork.

A mass design for summer flowers, by Julia Clements. The urn-shaped vase was filled to above the rim with crumpled chicken wire. Tall delphiniums in the centre were flanked by tall stocks with shorter stocks and sweet peas tilting forward. Richly-coloured roses were placed down the centre and leafy twigs at the back below the stems united the design

Another lovely mass design, this time of dahlias mixed with sprengerii. The tallest blooms are used first and inserted in the centre. Flank them right and left with flowers gradually decreasing in size and then fill in the lower part of the design. Let some flowers tilt down below the rim of the container. As a final touch, use sprays of dark foliage as a background

The design is beginning to have form and meaning, for with the outline and centre fixed you are more than half-way to success.

The next step is to fill in with flowers of varying lengthened stems. Always avoid a "flat" arrangement by making your flowers flow out of the container. This is best achieved by placing the flowers at the front and side horizontally, with the others at different angles but all flowing from the centre.

Never place two flowers level with each other and remember that your finished design will always be artistic if you use groups made up of different numbers. Flowers all in twos give an impression of regularity — almost as of soldiers marching — especially if they are of the same height, so use three here, two there and four here.

Many beginners find trouble when the stems cross. This can be overcome by placing the stem just where it should come out — in other words, if you want a stem to flow out from the side, it should not be pushed right through to the opposite side of the container, where it will take up space which you will require later, but cut to the desired length and placed, held by the wire, at the point from which you want it to flow.

Don't jam your flowers too closely into the container. Always arrange them lightly and loosely — so that each one has a breathing space. This is particularly important if you are using any flowers actually in bud — you must allow for the growth from bud to full bloom.

It is advisable to put the finishing touches to your arrangement where it will finally rest, for it is a mistake to arrange a vase when you are sitting down, and then when the arrangement is finished place the vase, for instance, on a high shelf. Remember too that wall vases are always viewed from below, so the flowers and foliage should flow out and down. Such an arrangement should never be made too tall, and trailing material should be included if possible.

One of the difficulties beginners often experience with a mass design is that they tend to get the actual balance not quite right for the container, and the whole arrangement starts to tilt forward. If this happens, try pulling the whole design back into place by hanging a heavy pinholder, or a strip of lead, on to a wire at the back.

Remember that your background can be vitally important, so almost before you start arranging your flowers, decide exactly where you intend to put your vase. It is usual to keep the larger, lighter flowers in the centre of an arrangement with the smaller, darker blooms at the outside. But there's no hard and fast rule about this, so experiment. If, for instance, you intend placing your arrangement against a dark wall, then you could emphasise the lines of your design by reversing this process — lighter coloured flowers forming the outline with the deeper, stronger colours or shades in the centre.

The Ideal Shapes

A formal, massed triangular shape is ideal for the centre of a table backed by a wall, while an irregularly shaped mass design (one which is shorter at one side than the other) is better for one end of a large table.

A classic mantel vase is most suitable for one or both ends of a mantelshelf. These vases are usually filled with plenty of flowers, the outsides being made to appear visually heavier and shorter, while longer fine trails of flowers or foliage fall towards the centre and out over the shelf.

A bay window makes a lovely framework for a massed flower arrangement, but it is not always flattering if the light shines through the stems. To avoid this, make sure that the flowers are thickly clustered, with blooms curving over the rim of the container and then clustering solidly together upwards and outwards to the outline — rhododendrons are ideal for this type of display.

Don't despair if you find branches are not the shape you require for the lines of your planned design. Much can be done by pruning branches to suit your ideas and many sprigs can be bent into lovely curves by stroking them with warm hands or by leaving them in a bent position in warm water overnight.

Massed displays can look enchanting if placed on a pedestal — or a small, slender table — in a large room, but to enjoy their full beauty they should if possible be viewed from a distance.

Roses, of course, are a traditional choice for a massed or formal arrangement. There was an idea at one time that roses should be arranged only in cut-glass or silver, but this has changed now, and many delightful and interesting arrangements can be seen in all kinds of containers. A wooden container is eminently suitable while some kinds of pottery are ideally suited to the large roses, such as Peace; the old-fashioned varieties of roses are charming in old china vases and jugs; and, of course, the conventional cut-glass or silver, sparkling with good care, does enhance their beauty.

Colour is Important

Try to choose a container which is suitable in size and colour for the roses you are using; a large vase is better for the larger type of bloom. Remember that the colour of your flowers can be accentuated by the use of a container which either contrasts or harmonises with it. Yellow daffodils, for instance, look most attractive in a black pottery vase. Mimosa — a popular choice during the winter months — is another flower which looks delightful in a black glazed pottery vase. (Days can be added to the life of this fragrant blossom by re-cutting and steeping the stem ends in almost boiling water, and by then adding a little granulated sugar to the final arrangement.)

Upright and urn-shaped vases are excellent for massed displays of any blooms. When buying new ones it is important to pay attention to colour, remembering that they must not only combine well with your flowers but also blend with the colour scheme of your room. Baskets, which are generally neutral in colour, make admirable containers for autumn arrangements. Your local florist should be able to supply suitable ones, or your own shopping basket would do if lined with tin.

Colour can be very important. Some shades are termed warm and advancing, while others are called cool and receding. Red is stimulating and is grouped with vibrant orange and gay yellow — have you noticed how yellow and red flowers demand your attention the moment you enter a room? It is for this reason that these colours are often used at, say, chattering cocktail parties, while pale pink, apple green and mauve are better choices for a more intimate dinner party or gathering. Blue, incidentally, fades almost to grey-black at night, so blue flowers are better avoided if your evening lighting is very soft.

It could almost be said that we "speak" with the flowers we use. To say a happy, gay welcome, lighten the entrance hall by using yellow, flame or coral flowers in a mass design on a hall table.

Here is an example of a classical, or formal, design. In this small but lovely arrangement, white Magnolia Campelli has been used in both bud and full bloom. The goblet shaped silver bowl is complimented by leaves of Silver Ornipodium which give body to the design

*A beautiful profusion of lilac and azaleas in vary-
ing shades sweep over the rim of the container.
Note how, although there is a distinct right and
left to this design, yet the whole merges into a
glorious blaze of colour. Before arranging, all the
woody stalks were hammered at the end, stripped
of their foliage and placed deep in cold water*

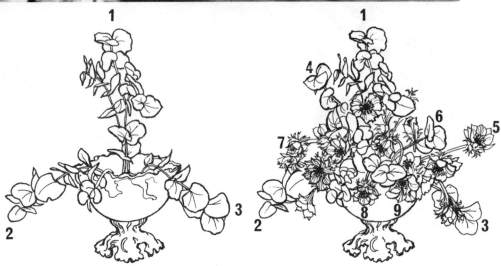

Anemones may seem too humble for a mass design, more suitable perhaps for a simple posy but, as you can see from our photograph, they can be made into a charming display. Their vivid colours stand out beautifully against eucalyptus foliage. Follow our step-by-step sketches for arranging a triangular mass design. Place your tallest spray of leaves in position (1), and follow with the two corners of the triangle (2,3). This gives the basic outline. Then fill in with anemones, as in the second sketch. Leave the flowers curving over the rim of the vase (8,9) to the very last of all

A graceful display that, with the help of our sketches, is very easy to arrange. Early chrysanthemums make a diagonal line of colour in this design of lily-of-the-valley, freesia, carnations and foliage. Start with the tallest spray (1) and then with the base corners of the design (2,3). Two tall carnations go in next (4,5). Cut the stems of the chrysanthemums into varying lengths and insert them (6-9). Finish off the outline with trailing sprays of freesia and foliage (10-15) and block in the centre of the design with some more freesia, as necessary. Two stems of freesia may be tied together for support

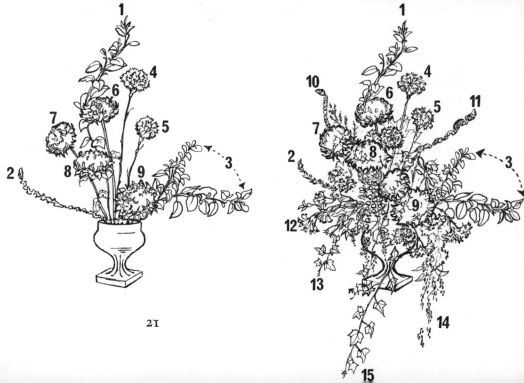

In the living room on a hot day, green, blue or white will produce a cool effect.

White flowers mixed with others are often difficult to place, for the white is often over-dominant and too eye-catching. It is best to place the white ones near the centre at a point beneath the tallest stems, or where all the stems are unified. This need not apply, of course, when using white flowers with green foliage only, which is a lovely combination. Green is always a stabiliser.

Floral colours don't clash, so you can mix your colours as much as you like. But you will find that massing flowers in blocks of colours is more effective than scattering different colours throughout an arrangement.

If you are decorating for a party, it's always a good idea to try and pick up the colour scheme of

the room. It may be that you can accentuate the colour of the curtains, or your arrangement might be planned to harmonise with the furniture or some dominant object in the room. Don't forget that if the room is large and fairly high, a large mass display will be ideal, as it will not dwarf anything else. If you are planning for a corner, then you will want a taller and more formal design.

A difficulty which beginners often come up against is to see their beautifully arranged mass design wilting almost before their eyes. To avoid this, if you are lucky enough to have a garden, try to gather most flowers after sundown, when evaporation is at its lowest. Leave them in a bucket of deep water in a cool, dark place overnight before arranging them.

If, when you buy your flowers from the shop,

Left: Flowers are not easy to gift-wrap but bows of wide ribbon threaded through roses and carnations transform them into a lovely present for someone in hospital or for a very special anniversary

Above Right: A gay, glazed pottery vase echoes the spring effect of freesia, with blooms both fully out and still in bud. The small-leaved foliage enhances the whole impression of delicacy

Right: Simple garden flowers can be transformed into charming arrangements. Here, ordinary daisies carefully displayed and complimented by a gay pottery jug bring spring right into the house

you cut the stems slantwise and strip off the lower leaves you will find that the hours of deep drinking will harden the material and help it to stand stiff and strong the next day. Do exactly the same thing for garden flowers.

The surfaces of leaves are covered with pores and water evaporates from these pores in the form of vapour. That is why if a number of leaves are left on the stems they absorb the water first to replace their own loss and this consequently delays the water from reaching the bloom, which is usually at the very top of the stem.

When either cutting or buying flowers, always choose ones that are not yet fully developed, as these will grow and develop to their full beauty. Fully developed flowers will not last as long but may be suitable — and cheaper — for a special "one occasion" use.

All single flowers should have the centre eye in a hard, "greeny" condition. Daffodils and narcissi should be firm and crisp; roses and tulips closed and "buddy". Carnations should not show their centre white stamens. Only two or three of the lowest gladioli flowers should be open.

Don't buy the very tightest buds, but rather ones which are just showing colour. Freesias, which should be bought in this state, will last longer if you keep pinching off dead blooms.

Anemones in bud are an absolute must for they open particularly quickly in a warm room. Anemone stems, like tulips, should have no discoloured ends. Keep them cool if you want them to last longer. You can even put them in a frost-free cellar overnight to keep them fresh longer.

Iris, bought in bud, last longer too if you remove individual iris heads as they fade — this gives the lower buds a better chance to mature.

Hyacinths make good cut flowers. Many people transfer them from their pots to the garden after they have finished blooming, where they go on flowering year after year. They are not as fragile as you might expect. Buy them while they are still turning colour and be sure to let them have plenty of water.

Remember that different flowers have different expectations of life. Chrysanthemums, for instance, will often last a full three weeks, while dahlias do well if they last a week. Generally, autumn and winter flowers last longer than spring and summer ones. Flowers that are available almost all the year round last better than the ones which are with us for only a short season.

Flowers grown from bulbs are not heavy water drinkers — provided you have plunged them into water before starting on your arrangement. But check the water level in your container a few hours after arranging to be sure that your flowers are not thirsty.

Remember that there is no need to change the water in the vase every day — flowers do not take kindly to a lot of handling — it is quite sufficient to top up the water daily.

Strip off the leaves from the stems of all woody-stemmed flowers, such as roses, lilac, philadelphus, rhododendron, etc, as they are so absorbent that the water is prevented from getting to the actual bloom in sufficient quantities. If you like, you can always use the leaves separately in your arrangement. Always split or crush the stems of woody material, to allow for a greater intake of water. In fact, it will help even more if a few notches are cut up the side of the stem or branch.

All flowers of the semi-woody variety, such as stocks, chrysanthemums, wallflowers and marguerites, should have the ends of their stems scraped and even split.

Tulips and lilac love a spoonful of sugar in their water — remember that tulips are always better the day after they have been arranged. Unless you want curves in the arrangement, keep tulips in deep water wrapped round with newspaper up to their heads before arranging them. This will keep them straight.

All the flowers with stems which exude a milky substance such as that which comes from the stems of euphorbia fulgens, poppies, poinsettias, etc., should, after picking, be steeped for a few seconds in about two inches of boiling water before being placed in deep, cool water. This treatment seals the stems, which can, however, still take in water above the part that has been sealed.

Once your arrangement is finished, make sure that the flowers are not in a draught, nor in line with any source of direct heat. If you put your lovely arrangement above a hot radiator or fire of any kind, it is not going to last for long!

In this beautifully balanced example of the mass style of flower arrangement, tall tulip buds create a basic shape, gentler stocks and antirrhinums, irises and sweet peas help to soften the outline and roses, with long and short stems and in various shades, give depth and focus. This arrangement was built up in a wicker basket container lined with aluminium foil and the stems firmly held by damp Oasis, eliminating the need for water. Notice how the curve of the handle is emphasised in the final shape of the arrangement, which is exactly twice as high as the basket. In the mass style, particularly, contrast is extremely important in the shape, texture and colour of the flowers

This is a mass design. Using roses and stocks with other garden flowers, it's easier to arrange than it looks if you follow the diagram. The centre flower (1) should be two-and-a-half times the height of the container. Set tallest stocks (1-5) in a pin-holder under wire, then fill in outline with some slightly shorter roses. Complete the shape with irises, and some more fairly short stocks and roses. Add carnations (6,7) and groups of freesia

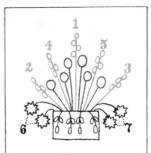

This is a formal design – simple and elegant – but this time using only stocks and roses. Based on the classic triangular shape, step-by-step sketches on page 15 show you how to arrange your flowers – whether they're a bunch from the garden or blooms from the shop

Another variation on the classic triangular shape shown on page 15. The spiky leaves of gladioli combine with the formality of carnations to produce an elegant arrangement. Chrysanthemum foliage at the base of the design provides a strong touch of colour

LINE DESIGN AND THE JAPANESE WAY

As distinct from Mass Style, which we discussed in the previous chapter, Line design is an arrangement of flowers, leaves, twigs, etc., where special attention is paid to the "line" or shape of the outline.

This style has been developed more recently than the traditional Mass Style and is growing in popularity all the time. It is really a fusion of Eastern and Western practice. The Americans, partly no doubt because of their close ties with Japan, have not only accepted the comtemplative Japanese style of arranging bare branches but have, by the addition of a few flowers, developed a style more in keeping with their own way of living.

If you live in a house or flat of contemporary design then you will almost certainly be extremely interested in this modern style of flower arranging. (This is not to say that because you live in an older house, or have traditional furnishings, that you are precluded from it; only that you are less likely to be attracted to it.)

Although appearing more boldly exciting that the traditional style, flower arrangements in Line Design are often easier to achieve and are certainly more economical in their use of materials.

A line design is usually, though not always, displayed in a shallow container with comparatively few flowers, having a linear theme for its basic principle. There are three requirements:

1. The quality of the material is of more importance than quantity.
2. The line to be illustrated should first be firmly fixed in the mind.
3. The design should be built up clearly.

Line arrangements are the quickest of all styles to execute, they are not complicated and you see the results almost at once. You will need a shallow container and to hold the flowers in place you should have one or more pinholders or a ball of crumpled wire netting fixed to the bottom of the container with plasticine. In every case the shallowness of the container will allow you freedom to place the flowers at any angle.

To get yourself started, try to visualise a line. It can be any line — a triangle, vertical, horizontal, right angle, a crescent, a Hogarth curve (a backwards falling S-shaped curve), an irregular triangle or even a fan. It may seem paradoxical to describe a curve as a line but you will see that curves form the basic outline of many of the actual arrangements illustrated in this book.

It really is most important to decide straight off which "line" to follow; then stick to it firmly when placing your flowers. Sketch it out first, if it helps. As a beginning, you may like to try the asymmetrical triangle.

To achieve this triangle, cut the first long flower or branch to one and a half times the height of your vase or, if using a low container, cut to one and a half times the width. Cut the second line to two-thirds the height of the main one and tip it out to the left at an angle of about 30 degrees. Then cut the third one to one-third the height of the first one and tip it forward and slightly to the right of an angle of about 45 degrees.

You can add more flowers to these basic lines, cutting the blooms shorter as they reach the centre but take care not to upset the outline, which should

These nine roses are set in an asymmetrical triangle in a beautifully patterned antique shell vase. The flowers are held in place by crumpled wide-mesh chicken wire. Right, above: a few blooms and buds of decorative spray chrysanthemums are held in a graceful crescent line design. Note the attractive container: an old silver biscuit barrel!

ultimately give your arrangement the three dimensions of height, width and depth. This effect is always pleasing, as it seems to invite one to look *into* the arrangement instead of just at it.

Try to add life or "motion" to your arrangement by repeating the line or by the blending of the colours. This may sound complicated in theory — in practice it is most certainly not complicated. If, for example, you start with pale pink flowers at the top of your design and work down with deeper colours, reaching perhaps a purple at the bottom, you can almost see the movement. The arrangement becomes alive instead of static. The same effect may sometimes be obtained by the graduation in the size of your flowers and leaves and in this respect you should use the smaller leaves and buds at the top, keeping

heavier leaves or larger flowers for the lower centre of the display.

After a little practice in visualising your line design before you begin, you may find that it is not only a mental picture of a line that will give you a start but possibly the unusual shape of a branch or the bold colouring of a flower. Sometimes a bold piece of woodland fungus may give you an idea or a pretty shell or polished stone on the beach. Often the shape of the container will suggest the whole scene, or an ornament might be your starting point. But whatever it is, let your creative powers have full play.

When you have progressed from making arrangements in the strict sense of "line", you will be able to graduate to more advanced arrangements by working from an idea or theme. Advanced

Above: yellow and gold roses are arranged here in a lovely free-flowing pyramid with variegated ivy leaves setting the main outlines. One leaf of begonia and one of philodendron mark the focal point of the design. Left: branches of blossom team with flag iris and a few anemones to make a colourful spring design. Right: the graceful shape of the basket is echoed in this gorgeous gift display. Fragrant roses and carnations blend with a few bunches of violets. They are held in wire netting in a painted pilchard tin hidden in the basket

Line Design arrangement may not exactly represent a strict line but it may suggest a scene or interpret an idea. As you absorb the principles of Line Design you will progress as an artist and, with abandon on some occasions and delicate artistry on others, you should be able to create the most beautiful pictures with flowers.

In bold Line designs you can attempt pure contrast in colours. Do not be afraid to use strong colours. If you are not sure as to what exactly represents a contrast in colour, try holding a coloured object, such as a book or a disc, against an off-white wall and then staring at it for some seconds. After concentrating on the colour, take the object away and the vision of a second colour will appear on the wall. This vision represents the colour contrast of the object. For instance you may find by holding up a red book that the colour that appears when the book is set down is green. Hold up a blue book and the secondary vision will be yellow. You could try using red

oriental poppies and green glossy leaves, or blue delphiniums and yellow snapdragons.

The correct colour combination of the flowers used will take you a long way on the path towards success.

The appropriate background is most important. If your walls are pale, you can place before them dark branches and bright leaves; if dark it would be better to use striking colours such as yellow, orange and scarlet.

The value of space in line design, too, must be realised and allowed for: be careful to resist the temptation to fill up the spaces in your arrangement because you are afraid it might otherwise appear too sparse.

Containers are an important consideration in Line Design. Ideally, they should be plain and uncluttered in appearance, perhaps made of thick metal, glass or pottery although again imagination can be given full rein. A flat board on which a design may be impaled on a pinholder, perhaps

Red single dahlias with a gold rimmed centre, Vicar of Llandaff, are blended into a colourful pyramid together with a few stalks of golden barley standing one and a half times as high as the width of the dish plus a few corn stalks at the base of the design. The flowers and barley are impaled on a hidden pin holder with a piece of aluminium foil to contain the water, or damp Oasis; a natural log, or (often used by experts) empty sardine or salmon tins make good containers. There is great fun to be found in looking for suitable containers. Second-hand furniture stores, antique (and plain junk) shops are happy hunting grounds for the ardent flower arranger!

Although flowers alone can make interesting modern line designs, a contrast of form will make the pattern more eye-catching. For instance, a tall branch with short flowers grouped low down, or tall flowers with a piece of gnarled wood placed low in the design, will prove more exciting than six flowers all of one kind placed upright.

With creative modern arrangement, it is never too soon to start looking for accessories, so useful for adding a different shape or form to your design. Collect some large stones, rough pieces of wood, old roots, dried fungus, shells, even ornaments, for all these are of lasting value. Pieces of wood can be sandpapered to obtain interesting textures and other items may be rubbed smooth, polished with shoe polish and finished in a variety of colours.

There are countless possibilities in the use of all kinds of flowers, buds, leaves, fruits, vegetables, twigs — including many items you may formerly have ignored. When you are able to get into the country, be on the constant look-out for any oddly shaped branch or unusual leaf and visualise them as integral parts of your composition.

Those who live in the country, or who have a large garden, may not realise the handicap confronting the flat-dweller whose precious flowers must always be bought, winter and summer as well. Tens of thousands of women who love flowers have to manage with few rather than abundance — for these women, particularly, Line design has much to offer, depending as it does on just a few flowers rather than a mass.

The Japanese Way

In Japan, flower arranging is a traditional art; in fact, it is more than an art, it expresses a philosophy of its own and requires patient study and wide knowledge to master it in its true form. Men as well as women devote years to its perfection and each of their creations is a poem in colour and shape, a declaration of faith.

Land is scarce in Japan and anything that grows naturally or is cultivated is treated as precious,

This striking line design consists of chrysanthemum combined with one spray of eucalyptus foliage. A length of crumpled wire netting inserted within the shell mouth of the unusual container holds the stems firmly in place and a begonia leaf keeps the wire netting hidden

In recent years, the Japanese way of flower arranging has spread to the Western world and, in a modified form, become as popular as the formal or mass style of arranging. American women, particularly, are extremely fond of this style.

To delve fully into the intricacies of the interpretations and symbols attached to the various Japanese schools of flower arranging would take a long time. In any case, few women have the time required for deep study and neither the philosophical education nor the inclination to sit for hours in contemplation of the finished design!

Basically, a Japanese line arrangement is built up around three main lines. They may be of branches or twigs but they *must* be in proportion to one another:

Shin, symbolising heaven, is the tallest and most important.

Soe, representing man, is of medium height.

Hikae, representing earth, is the shortest line.

There are also secondary lines, added after the main ones, known as *Jushis*.

The Japanese arrangement is usually built up from a flat container or a low, shallow dish. Flowers or foliage may be placed in position to accentuate the focal point of the design. They should be of varying height but none higher than three-quarters of the main line. *If* flowers are used, they must be used sparingly and each should be a perfect example of its species.

Ikebana, as the Japanese call flower arranging, has many schools of thought, including the *Sogetsu*, the *Nageira*, the *Moribana* and the *Ikenbo*. But each requires the three basic lines already described and each strictly adheres to the use of plant material in relation to the current season.

For instance, spring flowers would not be used with summer ones and material from trees or shrubs would be placed higher in a design than other flowers, just as they grow higher. A winter arrangement would be portrayed to give a sparse and withered effect; a spring design would be simple yet powerful in line, representing the force of early growth; summer arrangements would be fuller and more spreading, with additional foliage; while Autumn's theme would be thin and lean.

Here are two Westernised versions of the Japanese style of flower arranging. Above: a few shells, a few stones, a piece of driftwood and some tulips in bud are arranged on a flat board. The flowers and leaves are on a pin holder in a small vase well hidden. Below: five tulips, three in bud, are arranged with a twisted beech branch and leaves. The holder is hidden by moss and a stone from the beach

never used extravagantly. The same applies to the Japanese style of flower arranging. Beauty lies in its extreme simplicity, in the complete absence of any superfluity or clutter.

These two charming designs by Julia Clements show you how important a definite "line" is in any composition. Right, polyantha roses combine in almost oriental grace with leafy branches in a shallow, dark bowl. The longest branch should be one and a half times the bowl diameter

Below, garden flowers in a right-angle design which follows the line of the attractive basket container. Here flowers were made to flow over the rim of the container by inserting the last stems almost horizontally through the wire mesh which holds all the flowers inside the basket

Purple stock and broom thistle in an unusual arrange-
ment by Mary Dalgetty, of the Edinburgh Floral Art
Club. The piece of local granite is a clever touch - and
it also hides the pinholder fixed (with Plasticine) into
the small flat tin acting as a container. The whole
arrangement is set on a shallow stainless steel platter

Three magnolia branches in bud and one bloom are held in a pin holder.
The three candles stand in small holes cut in the curved side of half a potato

It is not easy for us in Britain to convey the sex distinctions to leaves and flowers as do the Japanese, with their infinite patience and highly developed techniques. They describe the front of the leaf as masculine and the underside feminine and therefore a considerable part of the art of their arranging is in the manipulation and twisting of the leaves so that equal amounts of both surfaces are shown.

In all Japanese refined arts, the importance of line predominates; and this appreciation of line, giving as it does the impression of motion and force, is the most distinguishing feature of their arrangements.

In order to avoid symmetry, which they con-sider very inartistic, the Japanese manipulate and prune branches to assume the required curves. Three, five, or seven lines form the basis of their designs, and all of these rise from one source in the container, as in natural growth.

It is possible to adapt a simple Japanese flower arrangement to suit our homes and the material we have available. All that is needed is a large shallow dish or plate, a flower pin holder, heavy enough to hold branches, and some stones or pebbles of varying sizes.

The exercise of creating a Japanese style line-design is all-satisfying and the feeling after completing a pure, utterly simple and starkly beautiful arrangement is of pure pleasure.

A beautifully balanced arrangement, left, is made up of five red hot poker flowers, iris foliage and hosta leaves and a most attractive piece of tree bark, smoothed and polished to show off its texture. Ideal for a round container

A crescent of roses, the queen of flowers! They need no other foliage than their own; start the design with the highest and the lowest leafy stems, placing them in crumpled chicken wire. Then fill in with blooms, largest to the centre, and more leaves

Above: an autumnal triangle for a complete change. The display consists of three stems of gladioli, pompom dahlias, stalks of dried wheat, bracken, nuts, berries, cones and two or three tree prunings. The material is held on a pin holder in a low dish

Right: A modified Japanese arrangement of branches, ivy and bright red leaves of poinsettia, including three flowers out in bloom

BASIC
PRINCIPLES

In the art of flower arranging there are certain basic principles which are common to all styles and which hold good whatever flowers or foliage are used.

Before starting an arrangement, make up your mind exactly how you want it to look. Decide on the type of container you will use (and incidentally, you can never have too many of these; the wider your choice of vases, bowls, baskets, copper ornaments and so on, the bigger the variety you can achieve with your arrangements).

Now decide in your mind's eye *the basic shape* you are going to work to. Will it be a Line Design or a Mass arrangement? The flowers will help you to decide this. If you have some large blooms to arrange like roses, carnations, chrysanthemums, etc., you may choose one of the solid forms for the arrangement, such as a big oval or a triangle; if, on the other hand, you are using tall, slender flowers like gladioli or stocks, you may want to arrange them in a triangle, a crescent or a flowing Hogarth curve.

Look at the position the arrangement will have in the room. A mantelpiece might call for a small, delicate arrangement; a side-table for a big, showy one. A low bowl, dressed so that it can be seen with equal pleasure from all sides, would be ideal for a coffee table; a rectangular design might prove a better complement to modern furniture.

Try to look at your setting as though it were a frame and compose your flower picture within this space. The frame, as you see it, may be one corner of the room, the dining table, the mantelpiece. Within the chosen frame, imagine the flo-

wers you have and, with a little practice, the design will come into your mind.

Having settled on the basic shape, keep it firmly in mind while you make up the arrangement. The next thing is to decide on the flowers you will use from those that are available, either to buy or to cut from the garden. It is much easier to choose when you know exactly how you want them to look.

To decide on the colour scheme of your display, consider these factors: the colours in the room, the position of the arrangement, the choice of flowers available and your own preference.

You can use colour in your arrangement in a number of different ways. You can achieve a feeling of gentle harmony by using two colours which are close to each other on the spectrum (the spectrum consists of all the colours you see in the rainbow, ranging through purples and blues to greens, yellows, reds. You can buy a colour wheel from any art shop to help you in your selection). Violet and blue harmonise, for example; so do red and orange. Often the best effect comes from using various tones of one colour. Or you can make your arrangement dramatic with contrasts – red and green or blue and yellow, perhaps.

The study of colour combinations for flower arranging is really most important for mass displays. However, in the creation of Line Arrangements, too, the correct colour combination of the flowers used will take you a long way on the path towards perfection in the art.

The distribution of colour in an arrangement

One of the simplest and most beautiful of all arrangement – daffodils, both buds and blooms, and irises, were cut to varying lengths and placed in casual-seeming profusion in chicken wire in a carved chalice container

can supply its vitality and motion. This may seem difficult to understand just at first and those who have in the past been accustomed to picking a huge bunch of flowers and thrusting it casually into a vase may even think that the suggestion of motion is unnecessary; but all the same it is quite true that you can almost visualise movement in an arrangement made with the accent on the graduation of colours.

In all cases, dark colours should be kept for the point of interest in the design, wherever it may be, and pale colours are best placed on the outside of the design. This even applies if you are making a monochromatic design, one of different tones of the same colour.

You may wish to create a display in blue, say, to suit a certain background; in this case you would start with the palest blue flowers and place these on the outside of the arrangement and then progress with flowers of slightly deeper shades until you insert those of the very deepest blue low down at the focal point to unify the whole composition.

Having made all these decisions – after a few arrangements they will be second nature, you won't consciously have to think about them – you are now ready to start work. Place your pin holder in the container, with some plasticine beneath to keep in it place. If the container is a deep one you may need to use some wire netting as well; otherwise just use the pin holder alone. You will need some Oasis or Florapak if you want to provide a "bed" for flowers in a basket or on a flat board.

Take the flower which is to be the main stem in your design, and cut it so that the part of the stem visible above the rim of the container is at least one-and-a-half times the container's biggest measurement (if a vase, this will be its height, if

A long, curving branch of yellow forsythia is the main line in the tall arrangement, left. The shape was suggested by the curving vase. The daisies and shiny-leaved foliage are also repeated in the complementary design, far left

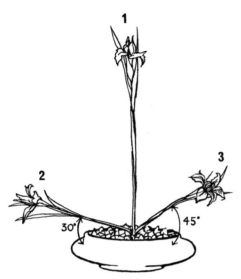

The asymmetrical triangle is built up in a low bowl from three main lines. No. 1 is 1½ times the breadth of the bowl and stands in the centre. No, 2, ⅔ of No 1, is tipped to the left at an angle of 30 degrees. No. 3 is about ⅓ the length of No. 1;

tip it forward and slightly to the right of an angle of about 45 degrees. Then fill in the arrangement with flowers and foliage, taking care not to alter the basic shape of the outline by placing this material to stand above the three main lines

Dahlias of all varieties are most rewarding blooms to arrange. A shallow glass vase, right, has been filled with chicken wire in which the flowers, berries, leaves and foliage have been firmly placed. Note the varying length of the dahlia stems; this is the first golden rule for the student to learn

a bowl, its breadth). Don't forget to allow for the piece of stem that will be hidden in the container. Place this main line where you want it.

Now take the other flowers, cut their stems to varying lengths (keeping them all shorter than the main one) and set them in the design so that they radiate from one central point. No stems should cross others where they are visible.

Make sure that the foliage you are using is correctly placed as a background to the blooms and to fill in and carry on the shape of the design

If you have planned a triangular outline, put your main line (one-and-a-half times the container, remember) in place first, in the centre. Your next line should be two-thirds as long as the first; tip it out to the left at an angle of about 30 degrees. Then cut the third line to about one-third of the

first and tip it forward and slightly to the right of an angle of about 45 degrees.

You can add more flowers or foliage to this basic outline, remembering to cut the blooms shorter as you reach the centre of the design; but take care not to alter the basic shape which should ultimately have a three-dimensional effect of height, width and depth.

Never be afraid to place your material horizontally (or even lower if the design calls for it). If your holder has been placed, *high* enough, the flowers, twigs and foliage will be held firmly at the desired angle. Probably wire netting is the best holder for horizontal stems although pin holders and Oasis will hold lighter, shorter material.

When it is finished, the whole arrangement must be firm and strong: it must neither topple

DO *use and keep your balance! One side is filled with daffodil buds newly bought; the other holds blooms from the buds bought the previous week. This design ensures a continuing and changing display of floral art. The blooms and buds here are held in Oasis which was first soaked in water. The design was completed with dark green foliage – ivy, for instance – and some sprays of honeysuckle*

over nor look as if it is going to. In the same way, it must also be perfectly balanced visually, so that it delights and satisfies the eye. To do this, you need to make proper use of the colour, the size and the shape of your flowers and leaves.

Dark, rich colours attract the eye more quickly than light, delicate ones, so the visual centre, somewhere near the base of your arrangement, should feature these "heavier" colours. Similarly, big blooms and leaves have more "weight" than small or feathery ones; use these weightier ones to lead the eye to the focal point of the arrangement.

The container, which is an integral part of any arrangement, should also maintain the balance. A big array of flowers in a small or flimsy-looking container will seem top-heavy; a small and pretty arrangement in a tall or big container will be

DON'T *forget that a display must follow a definite pattern – the shape is immaterial so long as it looks planned, which this example obviously was not. The flowers here all tilt to the left, they look as though they will eventually fall out of the bowl! The leaves, too, serve no purpose but have been placed haphazardly through the arrangement. The obvious thing to do with a bowl of jonquils like this is to lift everything out and start again completely from scratch*

A pyramid of lovely mixed blooms, leaves and branches shows how movement is introduced into a display solely by the use of colour. The darker, weightier tulips outline the main shape of the arrangement while the lighter blooms and the feathery foliage carry the eye precisely from one point to another in the design. From this, too, you can see how, by the clever use of a floral arranger's accessories such as crumpled wire netting and pinholders, a shallow container can still hold a mass display perfectly and not be top-heavy

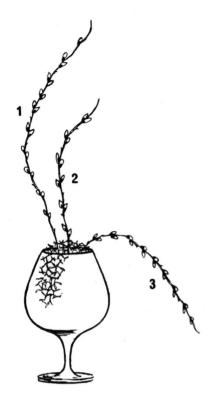 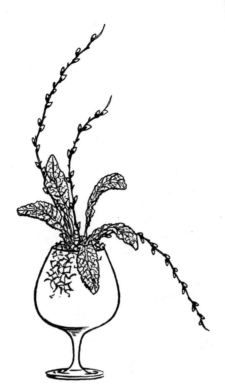 

These step-by-step sketches show how a simple but most effective line design is built up in a brandy glass, preferably a coloured one so that the stems are concealed. The glass is filled with wire netting and the first

line, 1½ times the height of the glass, put in place. (Don't forget to leave an extra bit of stem which will be hidden.) Lines No's. 2 and 3 are ⅔ as long as 1. Five primula leaves come next to hide the hard rim of the glass.

Finally, to give focal interest, a half-opened rose is placed in the centre of the display and one or two short pieces of rose foliage complete the effect. This is a most satisfying design to build up and capable of infinite variation

dwarfed. The container should also tone with the colour of your flowers or set them off by contrast. It is important, however, to be sure that the container is not so obtrusive that it draws the eye away from the arrangement itself.

Finally, avoid being too symmetrical in your arrangement. Try for a composition of graceful curves that balance each other, just as an artist does. Be as self-critical as if you were painting a picture. And increase your enjoyment by continually trying new designs.

To sum up, here are ten pointers to successful arranging:

1. Practise your arranging as often as possible.
2. Shape your design in your mind first.
3. Choose a container of the right size, shape and colour to give a balanced appearance.
4. Cut the main stem to show at least one-and-a-half times as long as the container's greatest dimension.
5. Place the stems so that they radiate from a central point but do not cross one another above the rim.
6. Use colour for gentle harmony or dramatic contrast.
7. Keep your "heavier" colours for the base and centre of the design.
8. Balance flowers and leaves according to size and shape.
9. Use foliage to set off the flowers and fill in the design.
10. Aim at rhythmical graceful curves that please your eye.

Finally, the most basic principle of all, remember that *enjoyment* is the key word. These pointers are to get you going and to guide you but most important of all is the pleasure that you and your family can get from your floral decoration. If an arrangement pleases *you*, you have made a success of it.

Dahlias again, here in an exotic autumn arrangement combined with dried seed heads, berries and tall dark brown bull-rushes. The classic urn container was first filled with 2-inch chicken wire to hold the stems firmly where they were laid. If the wire is inserted to come just over the rim of the container, stems can easily be placed horizontally

Right: a study in colour tones. Purple buddleia outline three deep mauve flecked dahlias in a stoneware jug. For an absolute contrast in display, a Lurex drape creates an impressive effect. Crumpled chicken wire with cut edges bent over the edge of the jug holds the whole arrangement firmly in place even when the jug is moved to another place

Left: Another lovely autumnal arrangement. Variously coloured zinnias form the body of this display, while the verbena and bull-rushes give a delightful graceful outline. Bunches of rowan berries and some small, bright crab apples make a vivid splash of colour nestling in the hollows of the unusual and attractive shellshaped container

Left: ten spray chrysanthemums in white provide a bright focus in this simple-looking yet most effective line design. It has been built up in a most realistic earthenware "log" and a pin holder holds the flowers and colourful beech leaves in place. Beech leaves are easy to preserve if picked at the right time of year. See "Dried Flowers"

Top right: a dramatic asymmetrical triangle has been created here with five large and lovely pale pink peony flowers and seven stalks of foxgloves. Queen Anne's lace and a few nicely pointed leaves have been added to the main material to provide a contrast in texture. The dainty figurine completes the effect

Right: An unusual and effective combination of flowers, grasses and foliage in the basic triangle shape. Tall thin sword leaves, quaking grass and iris seed pods provide height and grace while lilies and stephanotis add freshness and colour to the display. The use of artichokes provides body and interest, with leaves of plume poppy forming the base

In spring, watching the new buds open to full bloom is a yearly joy after the long, flowerless days of winter. In this arrangement, bright tulips have been chosen for impact and placed in a delicate and elegant framework of silver-grey santolina and lavender. Note the shallow container; bulb flowers do prefer shallow arrangements. The holder is a pinholder, held firmly in place by a little piece of plasticine

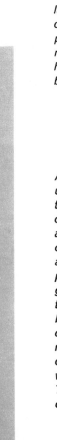

A graceful pyramid design uses just three different types of flower — gladioli, carnations and roses, plus a few sprigs of fern and one gladioli leaf to make a beautifully balanced display. The erect and formal gladioli are in perfect contrast with the rounder blooms of the roses and the carnations, while the dark rose shades and the lighter carnations and gladioli provide movement and vitality. The bow of ribbon tied low, on the right adds interest

Beautiful effects can be obtained by using only one kind of flower. Here, sweet peas have been formed into a triangle of delicate colour and set in a glowing copper bowl. On page 15 you will find step-by-step pictures showing how it's done

Another lovely design with only one kind of flower – but this time two shades were used. Arranger Jean Fread won a flower arranging contest at eighteen, which sparked off enthusiasm for training as a florist

CONTAINERS

The vases for either flower or plant arrangements should be chosen as carefully as the flowers themselves are chosen. It will never be possible for the finished effect to show to the best advantage unless the size and colour of the container is in complete harmony with the general design of your arrangement.

Most of us have seen lovely arrangements marred by the use of the wrong container. It is important to remember that line displays need a different type of container from that needed for mass displays. Line arrangements invariably need low, shallow dishes which have the advantage of displaying a few flowers effectively. Shallow bowls, plates of all kinds and even trays, if used with imagination, all have their uses.

We nearly all have a few upright and urn-shaped vases, and these are always best for mass displays. When buying new ones it is important to pay attention to colour, remembering that they must not only combine well with your flowers but also blend with the colour scheme of your room.

But, in fact, no keen flower arranger ever possesses enough containers to express her ideas fully. She needs so many receptacles of different kinds that although the art of flower arrangement will open her eyes to the beauty, colour and texture of glass, pottery and metal, just as surely it will eventually lead her to the necessity for making her own containers.

Tall cocoa tins are very effective when covered with Fablon or painted with a mixture of sawdust and paint. The sawdust gives a rough finish and, if finally lightly brushed over with a different coloured paint, the little rough pieces will stand out in relief.

A tall container in the classic pedestal style can easily be made by fixing a wooden bowl or tin to the top of a chair leg (many household stores stock these). The other end of the leg is then nailed to two square blocks of wood – one four inches square, the other three inches square – glued to each other. Paint with a matt paint; by rubbing this over with bronzing powder from an art suppliers an antique or marbled effect can be achieved.

Another idea is to paint a wine glass with frosted or pearly nail varnish. Filled with dainty spring flowers, the effect is delightful.

A mixture of black and aluminium paint will give a lovely antique finish to many a discarded vase, while well shaped, flat pieces of wood covered with Fablon make interesting bases.

Old mahogany tea caddies or work-boxes look most effective when filled with plants, as do old-fashioned corner wash-stands and bric-a-brac brackets. Tankards, vegetable dishes and wine bottles make excellent containers, while many of the modern vases, difficult for flowers, assume an importance of their own when filled with a plant.

Baskets of all kinds have many uses. The half-moon shaped shopping baskets make ideal containers, especially if trailing ivy or tradescantia is added. Indeed, old fishing creels, hampers, waste-paper baskets or even basketwork handbags become attractive containers for flowers, leaves and berries by lining them with a waterproof tin or dish.

Shells make interesting containers for either cut flowers, foliage or growing plants. An empty shell backed with sea-fern and grasses can dominate an arrangement; and if you place sprays of grey artemisia or pink Rose Bay willow herb (gone to seed) on a pin-holder set in the base of an up-turned clam shell, they can give the impression of plumes waving in the sea.

Placing a shell on a black wooden base or small tray will protect your furniture as well as adding

Wall vases are always viewed from below so, for the best effects, make sure that you arrange the flowers in them to flow over the rim and gracefully downwards. You will find foliage and a few grasses are a great help

to the picture. The large pale green snail shells, iridescent on the outside and pearly inside, are so jewel-like on their own that they need only a few tall, fine green sprays. Small shells of any kind, thrown around the base of a pin-holder in a shallow dish of water, make interesting underwater decorations.

Ordinary scallop shells can be grouped together as a table centrepiece. Make a pile of thick plaster filler powder on a base, inserting perhaps five scallop shells in a circle low down, then

So many different styles of containers – and yet each one is perfect for its own special type of floral display. If you are in any doubt about the right lines to follow in arranging flowers, display them to follow the basic curves of the container – then it's impossible to go wrong. With the exception of the little Venetian glass vase, all these containers were supplied by Cocquerel's, and are obtainable from high-class florists everywhere

three slightly higher at intervals rather like the petals of a flower, finishing with one at the top. Fill each shell with a small sedum or echeveria.

Stone cider and pickling jars combine well with fruit, wheat, foliage and berries for autumn arrangements. They have a tremendous appeal when placed on old oak dressers or other country backgrounds. Another lovely type of container for this kind of arrangement is a log of Silver Birch which has been hollowed out and lined with tin. Beech wood treated in the same way is also very attractive.

A natural wood effect can easily be given to tins of any kind. Mix a little cement with either clear varnish or flat or glossy paint – using any colour that is desired. A dull brown gives a useful rough wood effect.

To vary the surface texture, imprints of buttons, etc., can be made, and the appearance of ridged wood can be achieved by stroking the outside of the painted tin with a fork before the cement sets.

Pastel coloured effects can be obtained by covering tins with a mixture of Polyfilla – the white

A selection of typical modern containers. The bowl containing roses is in a style that has been consistently popular since Victorian days. For the best results, pinholders or crumpled wire netting which comes either above or right up to the rim should be used in these vases

plaster powder – and a dye or a few spots of coloured ink. You could try painting an ordinary kitchen colander with mauve paint made in this way, filling the holes with Polyfilla, and planting it later with pink and purple petunias. This could be hung on a coloured cord over a door.

Baking tins or pie dishes can also be transformed into attractive containers for flowers. They can be painted black, aluminium or bronze, and used by themselves, or they can be given greater importance by being fixed on to a base. For instance, on a piece of wood about eighteen inches by twelve inches, cotton reels could be fixed to act as feet. Then on one side of this little table an empty tin can be screwed. Finally, to ensure that it is all completely waterproof, put a second, slightly smaller, tin inside the first one. Coat the tin with vinegar and let it dry (this helps the paint to adhere) and paint the whole container black.

Candle Cups are a clever way of arranging a wide display on top of a slender vase or even on top of a wine bottle. They can be bought from a florist, or you can make your own. Screw a cork to the centre of the underside of a tin pie dish, drop candle-grease or sealing wax round the cork to prevent any leakage of water, and insert the cork into the neck of the bottle or vase. Make sure you weight the vase first by filling it with water – plain if the glass is coloured or, if the glass is plain, add a few drops of coloured ink to the water for a pretty effect. Short-stemmed flowers with downward curving foliage look best in this type of container.

Containers for plants can be delicate or coarse – glass or silver for maidenhair ferns, and pottery

Delightful for side table or top of a baby grand piano. Quaking grass and dahlias with a little darker foliage complement the lovely urn-shaped pedestal container

or wood for heavy leaves and for seedheads. Baskets are good for a mixed group of plants. Copper, brass and pewter are often the best choice for leaves and plants of similar colouring. A plant of silvery grey Stachys Lanata transferred to a pewter mug can make an inexpensive and appealing decoration on a bureau or a bookcase.

If you are in any doubt about arranging flowers or plants in any kind of container, always remember to follow the line of the design of the container. For instance, if it is curved, then follow this curve; if it is jug-like, think of the pouring function of a jug and make the design higher over the handle, flowing down over the spout. In this way, you will never go far wrong.

An old-fashioned knife box makes an attractive "shelf vase". Separate pots of water simplify line arrangements like this one. Pinholders, hidden by leaves, hold the stems firmly in place

Small decorative antique dishes – such as snuff boxes, bon-bon and confiture dishes – when well polished, make delightful containers for short-stemmed flowers held in place by a pinholder

This unusual display of autumn seed heads, quince fruits, foliage and Scotch thistle has been arranged in a candle cup inserted into the neck of a Dimple Haig bottle. To hold the heavy fruit and tall foliage firmly in place both chicken mesh and a pinholder were used

to contain... to be capable of holding

This lovely shallow bowl is made of glass. Milky white and shiny black combine to form a perfect setting for any display. Here, dahlias in various stages of bloom and also in different colours were used. With a shallow container like this one, a pinholder hidden under a little foliage – or by attractive stones by a little moss – is an absolute necessity

Freesias – which can be pricey – look as beautiful in small bunches as in quantity. Here they combine with a candle to create a festive atmosphere. The flowers were arranged in a basically triangular design, held firmly by a pin holder in a special candlestick "cup"

Above: another way with freesias; again the design is basically triangular but here the flowers are held in damp Oasis covered with moss, in a wooden casket lined with foil. Below: fully opened anemones are arranged here with some attractive silvery foliage, such as senecio, in a graceful crescent. A small pottery jug like this makes an ideal container

Above: a brightly coloured arrangement of spiky sunflowers and anemones was made on a flat tin and pin holder concealed by the flowers themselves and also by plenty of foliage. Below: a charming Christmas decoration consists of some dainty marguerites arranged on a flat dish and pin holder, completed by a painted log, gold cones and leaves, silver balls

This is a typical example of the way in which the shape of the container suggests the line of the finished design. A shell, filled with crumpled wire netting, holds a group of Mrs. Sam McGredy roses, placed in a diagonal pattern following the opening of the shell. Start with the longest rose at the top, cutting the stems of the rest shorter to keep the pattern. Make sure that some flowers flow forward, to give movement. Arranged by Julia Clements

An unusual and charming container for hanging on a wall. Any shallow basket could be used like this one to make a pretty background for a floral display. The neutral shade makes a perfect foil for the coloured flowers. Insert flowers into a little piece of Oasis wrapped around with some aluminium foil

Peruvian lilies have been used in these two arrangements. In the taller vase, the lilies follow the lines of the actual container a trick which is always useful when inspiration fails to come! The smaller vase is ideal for either a line arrangement or a low, pretty cluster of flowers

MAKING
THE MOST
OF
A FEW

Look closely at any vase of flowers and you will see that whatever the style of arrangement it is also a collection of individual flowers and leaves. Each is perfect in itself and you will find that there is as much pleasure to be found in arranging and displaying one or two perfect blooms as in a bouquet.

Although, of course, you will still enjoy having bunches of flowers in your living rooms when they are easily available, don't be discouraged and give up your new-found hobby when material is difficult to obtain – in the winter, for instance, when gardens are bare and cut flowers expensive, or in spring when the first few flowers are bursting into life and to pick more than one or two would deprive the garden.

The whole art of arranging a few flowers is in the composition, the proportions of flowers, foliage, branches. After only a while you will be thrilled to discover just how many different ways there are in which to place five, three or only one flower to marvellous effect.

When you are faced with just one or two blooms and some foliage to arrange, it is very important first to decide exactly how you want it to look. With just a few flowers, your imagination has more play than with many. It may be the gold outline of a calla lily that suggests it should rise from a base of leaves, or perhaps you feel that five chrysanths would look particularly attractive in a simple vase, informally, just as they grow;

WOODLAND FANCY,
a delicate winter arrangement
Material: *a few sprays of ivy and some larger leaves; the flowers are Christmas roses. (You could, if you wished, substitute anemones for the roses.) You will also need a bare branch and some bark*
Know-how: *the bark and branch are held in place by plasticine, the flowers and foliage on a pin holder*
Arrangement: *Put the branch and bark into position first, then the three main ivy sprays. Cut the flower stems to varying lengths and put them in place before adding a few ivy leaves*

SPRING SONG,

a burst of colour on a grey day.
Material: *three anemones, a few narcissi, a few sprigs of broom*
Know-how: *broom can easily be curved into shape by stroking and shaping with the hand. And anemones prefer water to stand in rather than one of the modern porous holders*
Arrangement: *use chicken wire crumpled inside the container to hold the material. First put the broom sprigs into place at left and right; then place the three anemones in position along the centre of the container. Finally, fill in with a few narcissi blooms*

the planning of such arrangements is good mental exercise for you!

Japanese flower arrangers, of course, are past masters at making the most of a few. One perfect flower, perhaps three at the most, are all they allow themselves; and their designs are among the most beautiful in the world.

There are other ways in which to extract the utmost value from your material. Containers should be really clean to discourage the growth of bacteria. Incidentally, copper and other metal containers keep the water sweet and reduce decay.

Emptying vases daily and refilling them with fresh water is needless and sometimes harmful. Flowers do not like excessive handling. Initially,

the water in your vase should have the chill off before the flowers are placed in it. Then top up daily, again using water with the chill off.

All flowers will last longer if placed in a good light, though not in dazzling sunshine. Cut flowers should not be placed in draughts, nor near open, gas or electric fires.

There are endless possibilities if the mind is flexible, as you will see from the colour photographs between the preceding pages and the black and white pictures that follow. These are just a few ideas, there are hundreds more and no two alike – but only you can realise them and in doing so achieve the tremendous satisfaction that comes from making the most of a few flowers.

ORIENTAL SUNSHINE,

a modified Japanese line design.
Material: *a branch of pine or beech; chrysanthemum flowers and foliage*
Know-how: *the branch makes this; any shapely one will do and to perfect its line, remove some needles or leaves and prune away any unnecessary twigs or some of the side growths*
Arrangement: *use a low bowl and keep pin holder in place with plasticine. Insert branch firmly to one side. Use some foliage to hide the holder and set the bud and bloom into the focal position last of all*

OUTLINE INTO PAINTING,
*a display that changes as the buds
come into full bloom*
Material: *six tulips in bud and a
few leaves of bracken*
Know-how: *buy tulips in bud
– they are fresher, easier to arrange and will last far longer than
tulips bought when they are already in full bloom*
Arrangement: *the tallest tulip
(1½ times the height of the vase)
is inserted into chicken wire, then
the lowest, followed by the flower
leaning out to the right. Gradually
add the other buds and the bracken,
always emphasising the three-way
movement of the arrangement*

BOLD AND BEAUTIFUL,
a delightful spring arrangement
Material: *a few daffodil buds
and blooms; a few sprigs of pussy
willow; ivy leaves*
Know-how: *the perfect way to
arrange daffodils is in a shallow
container – in fact, all flowers
grown from bulbs prefer this type
and just a little water*
Arrangement: *fix some wire netting to a pin holder in a low,
and open container, cut the flower
and pussy willow stems to varying
lengths and place in position,
working from side to side and in
and out. Cover pin holder with
a few ivy leaves*

MADAME BUTTERFLY,
*an enchanting arrangement, giv-
ing an impression of the Orient*
Material: *a suitably shaped leafy
branch, such as beech; 2 rhododendron blooms*
Know-how: *the secret behind
this arrangement lies in the choice
of branch – you may have to
look hard before you find just the
shape you want*
Arrangement: *the material is
held on a pin holder fixed firmly
to the container with plasticine.
The branch is put in position first,
then the two blooms, the larger
of which should be placed low,
in the centre of the arrangement*

STILL LIFE,
*a design of leaves, delicate buds
and flower heads in glass*
Material: *a few clematis leaves,
spiraea and some flower heads
– such as anemones*
Know-how: *this is a very simple
arrangement, displayed in a low
glass dish. The pieces of glass
are sold especially for flower arrangements and give a cool effect*
Arrangement: *cut the stems of
spiraea and clematis to varying
lengths and arrange in the shape
of an asymmetrical triangle. Put
the glass pieces in the dish to
conceal the pin holder and then
carefully add the flower heads*

ROSES IN FOCUS,
a Japanese-style arrangement
Material: *a leafy branch and some driftwood; three roses*
Know-how: *simplicity is the essence of all Japanese-style arrangements. Remember the three main lines, Shin, Soe and Hikae (Heaven, man and earth) and arrange blooms in order*
Arrangement: *Put a pin holder and some crumpled chicken wire in a low dish on a board (you can buy these boards from any good florist) and insert the branch first of all. Cover the holder with foliage and place the roses in position. Finally add the driftwood*

A CHANGING PICTURE
for the first daffodil days.
Material: *daffodil blooms, daffodil buds; foliage (these are arum leaves but any well shaped leaves would do instead); some green bun moss*
Know-how: *the buds and blooms are arranged on opposite ends of the dish in similar designs and as the buds open and the blooms fade, more buds are used to prolong the display*
Arrangement: *the stems are cut to varying lengths and left in a little water for two hours. Then they are placed on two pin holders and packed in with moss. Foliage softens the container's edge*

THE SEASONS

Spring, summer, autumn, winter... each has its own special pleasures and delights. Every month finds something new in our gardens or the countryside, flowers or foliage which can be brought indoors and arranged to show their beauty inside our homes. Here, and on the following pages, are the names and some pictures to remind you of what is blooming when – and where.

SPRING

MARCH

Garden flowers in bloom

CROCUSES
DAFFODILS
ANEMONES
FORSYTHIAS
HELLEBORES – the Lenten roses
FLOWERING CHERRIES
OTHER SHRUBS, Camellias, Rhododendrons, Daphnes, Willows, Corylopsis, Pieris, Chaenomeles.

Wild flowers in bloom

PRIMROSES AND VIOLETS
WILD DAFFODILS
KINGCUPS
BLACKTHORN

APRIL

Garden flowers in bloom

DAFFODILS
HYACINTHS AND TULIPS
AZALEAS
RHODODENDRONS
MAGNOLIAS
FLOWERING CHERRIES
FRUIT BLOSSOM
LILIES OF THE VALLEY

Wild flowers in bloom

DAFFODILS
ANEMONES

WILD GARLIC
PASQUE FLOWERS
COWSLIPS AND OXSLIPS
KINGCUPS
BLACKTHORN
PUSSY WILLOW

MAY

Garden flowers in bloom

APPLE BLOSSOM
WISTERIA
LABURNUM
LILAC
TULIPS
AZALEAS
RHODODENDRONS
FLOWERING CRAB APPLES
FLOWERING DOGWOOD TREES
CEANOLTHUS
PRIMULAS
PEONIES
ALPINE PLANTS

Wild flowers in bloom

BLUEBELLS
BUTTERCUPS
GORSE
RHODODENDRONS
AZALEAS
MAY
SPRING GENTIAN
THRIFT
WILD ORCHIDS

PICK OF THE SEASONS

Spring. *A flower arrangement with all the freshness of these lovely months. The cleverly matched colouring of the hyacinths and irises blends with the delicate green of dieffenbachia exotica. The irises give height and delicacy, the hyacinth blooms give body and fullness to the design*

Spring. *Another charming arrangement – this time narcissus and prunus combine with coltsfoot, polyanthus and hosta leaves. Hosta is very easy to grow in your own garden, lasts a long time when cut and can be used in many ways*

Summer. *A delightfully distinctive design. Set in an ornamental white china tea-pot, pink and white carnations curve gracefully. The design has been given full prominence by being set on a side-table in front of a plain background*

Autumn

These months with their vivid floral colourings bring a wonderful opportunity for designs in a bright blaze of colour. Here, orange dahlias are clustered with some sprengerii in a plain vase inside a pretty basket container

Yellow cactus dahlias are set in a low cluster. Some stems have been cut very short so that the blooms cover the container rim. Always buy or pick dahlias before the centre cluster of each bloom is open, so they last longer

SUMMER

JUNE

Garden flowers in bloom

ROSES
DELPHINIUMS
PEONIES
IRISES
LUPINS
POPPIES
PINKS
CLEMATIS
RHODODENDRONS
AZALEAS

Wild flowers in bloom

ROSES
HONEYSUCKLE
WATER LILIES
POPPIES
MARGUERITES
IRISES
COW PARSLEY
WILD ORCHIDS
FLOWERS OF THE CHALK DOWNS
in June the chalk downs of the Isle
of Wight and behind the cliffs of
the south coast are gay with little
flowers; mauve scabious and yellow
rock rose, bright blue chalk milkwort,
little yellow St. John's wort and pink
centaury.

JULY

Garden flowers in bloom

LILIES
SWEET PEAS
OTHER HERBACEOUS PLANTS:
perennial phlox, heleniums, eriger-
ons, anchusas, gysophilas, lychnis,
lobelia, pyrethrums and potentillas.

ANNUALS; these are a feature this
month and borders are gay with a
great variety of annual phlox, annual
chrysanthemums, snapdragons (antirrhinums), petunias, marigolds, god-
etias, nemesias and many others.
SHRUBS, Escallonias, Buddleias,
Brooms.
ROSES

Wild flowers in bloom

TRAVELLER'S JOY, the wild Clem-
atis
WILD GERANIUMS
FOXGLOVES
FUCHSIA
SEA LAVENDER
RED VALERIAN

AUGUST

Garden flowers in bloom

DAHLIAS
GLADIOLI
OTHER HERBACEOUS PLANTS
HOLLYHOCKS
ANNUALS (see July)
SHRUBS
HYDRANGEAS
ROCK PLANTS
GERANIUMS
WATER-LILIES

Wild flowers in bloom

HEATHERS
ROSE BAY WILLOW HERB
PURPLE LOOSETRIFE
FIELD GENTIAN
GORSE
MEADOWSWEET
POPPIES
CORNFLOWERS

Far left, above: Spring – you can safely mix any spring flowers in any arrangements, their colours never clash. This simple design in a divided vegetable dish is composed of freesias, narcissi, primroses and lauristinus, all held on a pin holder

Left, above: Spring again – in fact, a daffodil simply sings of spring! Narrow vases are probably the most difficult of all to arrange flowers in; the secret is to vary the height of buds and flowers. And the attractive leaves in this arrangement are kale!

Left: the flowers that bloom in the spring are here in enchanting variety, arranged in a foil-lined basket on an Oasis brick. There are some brilliant anemones, crocus, tulip, narcissi and blue grape hyacinths

Above: spring tulips in a sea-shell – fill it with Oasis or Florapak first and cut the stems to varying lengths before inserting. These tulips were all bought in bud three days before being photographed

Above, right: Summer, and a bouquet picked on a country walk brings it right indoors. Wild flowers tend to wilt and should be left in deep water for a good long soak before being finally arranged

Right: Summer from the garden – these carnations and roses are held by Oasis covered with chicken wire, stems cut to varying lengths. Then they were placed "in and out" for informality and for balance

AUTUMN

SEPTEMBER

Garden flowers in bloom

DAHLIAS
CHRYSANTHEMUMS
MICHAELMAS DAISIES
HYDRANGEAS
BULBOUS PLANTS

Wild flowers in bloom

HEATHER
HAREBELLS
WILD FRUITS
SPINDLE-TREE
WAYFARING-TREE

OCTOBER

Garden flowers in bloom

DAHLIAS
CHRYSANTHEMUMS
HERBACEOUS PLANTS

GARDEN TREES AND SHRUBS
JAPANESE MAPLES
SORBUS

Fruits and foliage

COLOURED FOLIAGE
OLD MAN'S BEARD
HORSE CHESTNUT

NOVEMBER

Garden flowers in bloom

CHRISTMAS ROSES
WINTER FLOWERING VIBURNUM
STYLOSA IRISES

Fruits and foliage

COTONEASTERS, SORBUS AND
CRATAGEUS
WILD IRIS

Of special interest

Fine displays of berried shrubs may be seen in September at Kew Gardens, at Wisley, at Sheffield Park, Sussex, Westonbirt, Gloucester, Bedgebury Arboretum, Kent and Stourhead, Wilts. The Royal Horticultural Society's Great Autumn Show – a smaller version of the Chelsea Show for autumn flowers and fruits – is also held this month in the R.H.S. Halls, Vincent Square, London. In November comes the Late-flowering Chrysanthemum Show and the National Carnation Society's Show, also in the R.H.S. Halls. Topiary, the art of clipping shrubs into ornamental shapes, is practised in many gardens in Britain. It may be seen to advantage at Chaselton House, Oxfordshire, at Rockingham Castle, Market Harborough, Leicester, and at Hampton Court, Middlesex, where the Maze is world-famous.

Right: prunings from pine and fir trees together with berries and flowering shrubs make a charming display in a polished pewter tankard. The tankard was first filled with crumpled wire netting to hold the material in place. Below; warm autumn shades from gold to deep red in dahlias and gladioli follow a pattern through from top unopened buds to base. The heavy dahlia foliage balances sharp gladioli spikes. A dark brown container enhances the effect Below, right: massed triangle of autumn's flowers and fruit is arranged in a shallow goblet container. Note the subtle contrasts in the textures and shapes of the main flowers—roses, carnations, dahlias, and the focal bunch of rounded grapes

69

WINTER

DECEMBER

Garden flowers in bloom

CHRISTMAS ROSE
WINTER JASMINE
STYLOSA IRISES

Fruits and foliage

HOLLY BERRIES
MISTLETOE
IVY

JANUARY

Garden flowers in bloom

CHRISTMAS ROSES
SNOWDROPS
STYLOSA IRISES
WINTER CHERRY
WYCH-HAZEL

Wild flowers in bloom

PRIMROSES AND VIOLETS
WINTER HELIOTROPE

FEBRUARY

Garden flowers in bloom

WINTER ACONITES
SNOWDROPS
CROCUSES
EARLY DAFFODILS
IRISES and many other bulbous
plants, like dwarf cyclamen
CAMELIAS
EARLY RHODODENDRONS
CORNELIAN CHERRY

Wild flowers in bloom

PRIMROSES AND VIOLETS
COLTSFOOT
HAZEL CATKINS

Of special interest

The first flower show of the year is held towards the end of January at Vincent Square, Westminster, London, S. W. I., by the Royal Horticultural Society

Right: an unusual hanging display for Christmas is made on a cheap plastic mat; holly and Christmas tree prunings are fixed on firmly with wire, cones leaves and bells are added to complete the festive effect. The decoration is then suspended from the ceiling or can be hung on the wall

Below: winter warmth comes from the glowing red poinsettias and the one bright apple in the centre of this cheerful arrangement. Grapes and nuts, berries and ivy and prunings from the Christmas tree all go to give a look of plenty in mid-winter

71

ARRANGING CHURCH FLOWERS

BY MOLLY PUREFOY

The Church's year, beginning as it does in Advent, four Sundays before Christmas, finds us at the end of the flower season, and the change to a purple frontal on the altar calls for something different in decoration, or else none at all.

When the Sanctuary is very large, a pair of ball-shaped bay trees in tubs look very well, and they can stay in position until Palm Sunday, and so solve the flower problem for several months.

When the time comes for flowers again, the bay trees should be put outside in the churchyard, or in a garden to recover from their long sunless sojourn inside. They should be kept moist all through the summer, and when they grow new shoots these should be pinched back to two leaves, when they are three or four inches long – keeping the shape of the tree in mind as it is done. It is wise to give an occasional watering with a dried blood fertiliser, as the tubs get very full of roots, leaving little room for earth to nourish the tree.

A massed design of philadelphus – mock orange blossom. By stripping off the leaves the delicate blossom is left to contrast against the stone of the walls. This arrangement comes from Christ Church Cathedral, Oxford

SEASONS

LATE AUTUMN: Dahlias and chrysanthemums are what we rely on after the summer flush of flowers is over, and with the help of a cold greenhouse the latter can provide all that is necessary right up to Christmas. In order to save labour, all varieties of chrysanthemums can be grown in the open until the very end of September, when those whose buds are still quite small should be put under glass, either in a bed in the floor of the greenhouse, in large pots, or in old buckets. Here is a tip to prevent the plants from flagging after transplanting. A week before they are to be moved take a spade and cut a square round the roots to a depth of four or five inches. This teaches the plant to do without a wide spread of roots – and ensures that it has no check when moved. If the ground is dry, water the plants the day before cutting round them. Plants with more advanced buds can be accommodated in a light shed, and will come into flower before the frost is sharp enough to damage them. If a little heat is available, the season can of course be prolonged almost indefinitely according to what varieties are grown, but I must admit that by Christmas I am heartily sick of them and welcome the change to evergreens and then to spring bulbs.

Dahlias, of course, perish with the first frost, but they are so easy to grow and so generous

The beginning of the Church's year is Advent, but unfortunately December is a poor season for garden flowers. Small bay trees in tubs, however, like these in Tewkesbury Abbey, make an ideal church decoration until Palm Sunday. They can be supplemented around Christmas time with big jars or pots of variously coloured chrysanthemums

with their blossoms, that they make up for the shortness of their season.

A batch of gladioli planted in May will provide flowers in October, and these will make a lovely arrangement with Michaelmas daisies, which are inclined to look fussy unless they have some bigger flowers mixed with them.

CHRISTMAS: We all have our own ideas about Christmas decorations, but I personally like greenery only, except for a trimmed and lighted Christmas tree, but some people may like to provide flowers as well.

The best effect I ever saw was produced by some church decorators who, before Christmas, happened to be driving through a tract of country when the Forestry Commission was clearing an area of spruce. The woodmen had taken away all the trunks but had not as yet tidied up and, scattered about among the branches, were the tops of the trees, each about six feet high. These two people had great imagination and also an old Austin Tourer car – and they went back the next day and loaded it with the tree tops, and again the day after that. The result of this enterprise was that a tree was placed by each pillar in the Nave – making a miniature avenue – with one on each side of the High Altar. It was a really lovely sight. Such a chance would not come one's way often, but you never know what might happen, so pass the idea on in case it should ever occur again.

There is an old Welsh traditional Christmas decoration that can be adapted to the Font or the Chancel Screen, or even the table. Procure enough small oranges to go round or along whatever you intend to decorate, spaced about six inches apart. Cut enough five-inch twigs, from willow or hazel bushes, to make three legs for each orange and push them in so that it stands on a tripod. A few sprigs of yew or other evergreen are stuck into the shoulders of the orange and a fat white Christmas tree candle inserted in the top. The meaning is as follows:

The orange represents the World
The three legs – the Trinity
The evergreen – Eternity
The candle – the Light of the World.

Write the explanation clearly on a large card and put it near the decoration, so that everyone who sees it may understand its significance.

Arrangements for Christmas decoration can be done in exactly the same way as spring and summer flowers, using varieties of evergreens, fruit, cones and nuts instead: either in their natural colours or whitened with Tide suds or sprayed with gold and silver lacquer. Heavy cones had better be wired to twigs, as they are likely to fall off their own branches when they get warm and dry. Make your arrangement in a bowl or vase containing wire netting – using cones or nuts as the highlights.

There are so many different varieties of evergreens, ranging from the gold and silver of the cupressus to the lovely blues of various cedars, and deep greens of yew and ivy. Variegated holly can well be used as "flowers" with a background of the darker kinds.

I once saw a most effective Christmas arrangement done with shoots of Magnolia grandiflora which, in the late autumn, has cream coloured egg-shaped buds – though, of course, these have gone by Christmas. The lady who had done it had blown white eggs and used the shells as buds fastened to the centre of the shoots. She had painted slight shadings on the eggs, and even real gardeners were taken in and remarked that they had never seen magnolia so late in bloom! She told me that in order to have an unblemished point to the "bud", the blowing had to be done at the big end only. Make a hole, not necessarily very small, and push in a straw – making sure

that the yolk is broken. You then blow down the straw and the egg bubbles back out through the same hole. When the egg is empty, stick the middle inch of a seven-inch strip of Sellotape over the hole leaving the ends free, then put a short strip across the first, and stick it very firmly to the egg shell – the two free ends are then used to attach the egg to the centre of the magnolia leaves. Not only was this very original, but extremely beautiful, and remained so for weeks.

If you own bay trees, they can of course be incorporated in the Christmas decorations: jars of evergreens being grouped round the tubs, giving the effect of a little wood or shrubbery.

The Christmas tree takes pride of place, and can be trimmed with the usual glass and tinsel ornaments, or with apples, oranges and nuts hung on with black cotton which is threaded through them with a long needle. Coloured electric lights can be used with either of these schemes. In Tewkesbury we got a new, bigger, set of lights with Memory Money given by the friends of a man who had been devoted to children.

The Crib can be made in various ways. Some churches have a wooden stable ready made. In other places it is built each year with slabs of stone with a flat roof, or even rough stones to form a cave. Once I saw a threefold Crib in which the Shepherds were on one side, the Wise Men on the other, and the Stable further forward in the middle. This had been very cleverly lighted with a string of small Christmas tree electric bulbs, which had been taken out of their sockets, and rearranged so that the Shepherds and Angels were lit with blue and green to represent moonlight, with red ones for a fire – the Wise Men were coming across a desert in orange and yellow sunlight, and the white ones were concentrated in the Stable. It really was a masterpiece. Tiny vases of spring flowers, placed in the chinks of the stone-work, and Christmas roses, make a better decoration than evergreens. A palm in a pot can give an eastern touch – as also do a few small cacti or other succulents.

SPRING: Most churches dispense with flowers during Lent, but there have been times when we have had some bulbs still in bloom, and have allowed them to remain just to cheer up the people who

Large branches of elder flowers are wonderful in a corner or by a pillar – and they need cost you nothing! Look all around – for from the fields, lanes and even the bottom of the garden – there is so much you may have just for the cutting

Right: A lovely and simple arrangement that is ideal for a pair of vases on a small side altar. Cream-coloured violas and sprays of bluebells have been set in matching glass goblets

are just beginning to emerge again after being ill.

EASTER: Easter, of course, can be something of a problem, especially if it falls early and the spring is late. One way by which you can be certain of having some fresh greenery, is to bring chestnut sticky buds indoors about Midlent Sunday, and let them come into leaf in a warmer atmosphere. Forsythia and prunus can be treated like this too, so a little forethought can make a great difference to the Easter decorations. It is a poor year if there are just no daffodils about – though I think they are the most difficult flower to arrange. A certain amount of stiffness can, however, be taken out of them by holding the base of the stem in the left hand, surrounding the stem with the right hand and very gently running the

right thumb all the way up to the flower along the natural curve of the stem. One year we were given a quantity of really fine King Alfreds and one of our florists excelled herself by making an arrangement nearly four feet high with them. One of the iron urns was used, with sprays of laurel as a background. A green pottery flower vase was suspended from the tallest branch, and in this the top flight of daffodils was arranged. There are florist's tubes to be had which would solve this height problem – they are so light that several may be attached to one branch if necessary, and are certainly a good investment.

Arum lilies are often used at Easter – and although expensive to buy, do last several weeks and look splendid in any church, whatever the size. It is often difficult to get leaves to go with

them, unless one has some plants, and failing any of their own foliage, sprays of young laurel are, I think, far the best foil for them – or the big fan shaped Castor Oil leaves. If you do have the luck to get their own leaves, push a very long (20-inch) flower wire up the stem, and along the vein at the back of the leaf – you can then make them do exactly as you wish. I know a church where the members of the congregation are asked to give one lily each, and by this method there are lilies for all the vases, and no one has had to bear the whole expense.

Primroses brought by children can be lovely if only a suitable container is available in which to arrange them.

Gone, I hope, are the days when these flowers were stuck in jam or potted meat jars! Baking

tins can be used on windowsills, hidden by moss, and over-hung with branches of catkins, willow or any other pretty greenery to look like little trees.

Here in Tewkesbury we do our Easter decorations on Good Friday evening. The florists are invited to tea and eggs at the Vicarage immediately the Three Hours Service is over. At four o'clock everyone is busy arranging whatever flowers and greenery have been brought earlier in the day or on Maundy Thursday.

By seven o'clock in the evening the church is completely ready for the Easter visitors who come in on Saturaday morning, on their way to their holiday resorts. This plan leaves all the florists free on Saturday to do their own jobs at home.

WHITSUNTIDE: The colour scheme is red and

Sprays of pyracantha make a dark background for this lovely arrangement, which was especially designed to go on a pedestal in Gloucester Cathedral. A few peonies and three sprays of gladioli provide a focal point, while philadelphus – stripped of all its leaves – shines out against the dark background

A wide two-handled glass jug placed on a mahogany torchere makes a charming container for this lovely mass design. Using beech leaves as a foundation, lilac, irises and gladioli were all artistically mingled to produce this beautiful effect at St. Margaret's Parish Church at Northam, in North Devon

white, representing the Tongues of Fire that descended at the first Pentecost.

Usually there are early peonies, red poppies and pyrethrums available, and lots of white cow parsley in the hedges, which makes a lovely contrast to the heavier red flowers.

When making an arrangement of red flowers, be sure and include every possible shade of red. I know it sounds frightful, but I was given this advice by a very good florist, and you will see what I mean when you try it. Be sure to include scarlet and magenta, crimson and rose colour, and all the other shades you can find!

A patch of White Rocket in some out of the way corner is a great standby and is usually out for Whitsun, and lives well if picked young.

There might well be some Darwin or Cottage tulips available: in fact it is well worth planting a row of red and white ones (facing north to make them later). Choose the varieties that the bulb catalogue lists as late. Dutch white iris is also useful and easy to grow. Those who live in the parts of the country where rhododendrons flourish are generally well away with their Whitsun decorations.

Whitsun is followed by the long season of Trinity, when we have a green Frontal reminding us of the summer. Throughout this period flowers are plentiful and floristry easy – the one difficulty being that the church florists are apt to be away on holiday, so provision must be made to fill the gaps in their absence.

OCCASIONS

BAPTISMS: If decorations are to be done for

an individual christening by the request of the parents it is advisable that they should provide their own flowers, and help with the arranging of them. This does away with the pitfall of someone saying that the Font was decorated for So-and-So's christening but not for someone else's.

CONFIRMATIONS: Two bowls on pedestals look well when placed on each side of, and rather behind, the Bishop's Chair. They should be white or pale yellow – to blend with the white veils of the candidates.

WEDDINGS: Some brides are satisfied with whatever flowers are normally in the church, while others, more colour conscious, want them to match or tone with the dresses of their bridesmaids. In this case the flowers should be provided by the bride or bridegroom, and either ordered by them from the florist or money given to the person responsible for the flowers to lay out on the necessary material. In some places a picking patch is planted with bulbs or plants with money from the Flower Fund, in order to supply flowers for weddings and other occasions: the money received then goes back into the fund to be used again.

FUNERALS: When there are more floral tributes than will lie on the coffin, the remaining ones can be set on edge by the Chancel Screen or steps, or against the ends of the pews nearest the coffin, where they can be seen, but do not get in the way of the undertaker.

MOTHERING SUNDAY: An old custom, which is followed in many churches, is a family service at which the children are given bunches of violets to give to their mothers. One year, as violets were very expensive, I suggested to the Sunday School teachers that we should gather lots of snowdrops for the children to give instead, as we had sheets of them in the orchard. To my great surprise I was told in horrified tones that snowdrops meant death and how could I dream of making the poor children take them home to their mothers! I was astonished, for to me nothing could be a greater sign of new life than the snowdrops coming out of the hard ground – but evidently it is an old country belief.

PALM SUNDAY: Palm Crosses are often given by the church to members of the congregation on Palm Sunday, but if this is not done small sprigs of Pussy willow may be given to the children of the Sunday School to mark this day.

PLOUGH SUNDAY AND HARVEST FESTIVAL: Although not ranking as Feasts of the church, Plough Sunday and the Harvest Festival often bring a greater number of people to church than is usual on an ordinary Sunday. Plough Sunday is held before the flowers are out – a small sack of seed corn and a little group, near the door, of roots such as swedes and mangolds, with a few gay packets of seed, serve to remind us of our dependence on God to provide us with suitable weather to grow the crops that we are going to plant.

Harvest Festivals, of course, appeal more widely to country people, and village churches are often packed out for this service, and much produce from the garden is given with which to do the decorations.

One year we attended a Harvest Thanksgiving Service in an industrial town where there were no farms or gardens – the Vicar had so organised his congregation that everyone brought a tin of food as an offering, all of which he stored in a huge cupboard; during the winter he gave it away to the sick and poor of the Parish. I believe he had over a ton. I also remember going to London occasionally for weekends when we attended a church in a fairly poor district. When it came to the Autumn we were told that the Harvest Festival would be in a fortnight's time. When we went up again we took a few sheaves of corn with us and we found that it was the first they had ever had, and they were more than delighted with it. The children had never seen sheaves of corn before. Nowadays if you want to have sheaves of corn for the Harvest Festival, you must make arrangements with a farmer early in the season to cut some specially – or allow you to do it yourself – as practically all corn is now cut by a combine harvester and never gets into sheaf stage at all. But it can be arranged with forethought and co-operation.

REMEMBRANCE SUNDAY: With a little trouble, the British Legion poppies can be made into a beautiful arrangement with bay leaves and rosemary which will be a real ornament in the church.

And so we come to the end of the Church's Year.

This chapter is an extract from Molly Purefoy's delightful book, "Arranging Church Flowers", published by Pearson.

If you are thinking of exhibiting in your local floral show, study this lovely arrangement by Irene Hazell, F.R.H.S. Typical of good exhibition work, the flowers have been loosely arranged so that there is no over-crowding, and the soft variants of mauve and yellow blooms have been sensitively chosen and matched to blend into a harmonious whole

Try building up designs using various shades of one type of flower. Here sweet peas, ranging from white to deep red, have been gathered into a cradle-shaped china bowl

Here glowing red roses form the heart of a tri-angular design, with paler shaded roses on the outside. Before the flowers were arranged, they were stood in deep water and the stems were crushed. Both these designs are by Moyses Stevens

ONE
KIND
OF
FLOWER

If you are lucky enough to have a garden there will be times when all your efforts and hard work produce a glut of one kind of flower – daffodils, roses, dahlias... This lovely abundance demands all of your ingenuity in flower arrangements. The same problem occurs when flowers are inexpensive and you can buy bunches of seasonal blooms for little more than a few pennies. In this chapter we show you some lovely examples of designs made up from a single type of flower, and also give you some interesting facts about the chief varieties of flowers in this category

ANEMONES

With their vivid colours, these are among the prettiest and most inexpensive of flowers and have the added advantage of being in bloom when there are not many early flowers available. They are, however, somewhat difficult to arrange with their heavy, hanging heads. Use crumpled wire netting or a pinholder to hold the stalks firmly in place and always buy or pick anemones in bud for they open out into wide, saucer-shaped blooms extremely quickly. You can see some lovely anemone arrangements in the photographs in colour between pages 56-57.

CARNATIONS

For over three hundred years this has been one of the most popular flowers to be grown in English gardens, so the carnation has a strong claim to

Using yellow carnations in various lengths and green beech foliage, this design has been perfectly adapted to a pottery vase in that difficult, narrow tubular shape, by Mrs. Mary Muret, member of a Solihull flower club

our affection. There are so many varieties that one or other type is in bloom from spring to autumn. Border carnations can be grown from seed sown at the end of March or in early April. They have a whole season then to make their growth and will be in full flower the following season. Cuttings should be taken at about the end of September.

CHRYSANTHEMUMS

These lovely flowers are wonderful for both mass and line arrangements. Grown a great deal in Japan – a country which has had an enormous influence on the art of flower arranging – they are often used singly in line designs. Hardy chrysanthemums – such as Koreans and rubellums – come into bloom in late July and will keep the house gay until the frost. Kept at a tempera-

ture of 45-55 °F, cuttings should be planted in post any time from January to March and then planted out in garden borders from the end of April onwards.

CYCLAMEN

Another flower of which there are many kinds. Indeed, by growing only four different species of hardy cyclamen, you could have flowers almost all the year round. But the peak period for blooming is in the autumn. Buy small, growing tubers and plant very shallowly – only an inch of soil for covering. Cyclamen repandum has brilliant red flowers with long pointed petals and ivy-like leaves, flowers in the spring and has a sweet perfume. The neapolitanum variety is very useful to floral arrangers for, as well as its mauve-pink flowers, its leaves are extremely attractive – they

Right, a bunch of Valencia chrysanthemums arranged in a tall fountain-shaped design. The deeply serrated artichoke leaves give body, and all come from the centre — two being flung up and back for balance while the other two flow forward and down to emphasise the cascading effect.

Left, contrasting shades of carnations in a low container. A line of the darker blooms strengthens the centre and their spiky leaves form the outline

are marbled in pale and dark green – and from September will last right through the winter.

DAFFODILS

The golden trumpets of spring can be grown indoors or out, so that even those without a garden can enjoy these lovely blooms, which from the early days of this century have become more and more popular – probably because of the vast improvement in the quality of the flowers and the ever-increasing colour range. In fact, it is bewildering nowadays to make a selection from the hundreds of varieties offered. The King Alfred variety has been steadily popular for over fifty years but Golden Harvest is bidding fair to rival it with rich golden flowers and sturdy stems – it also flowers fairly early. A late-flowering daffodil is Unsurpassable, with large, deep yellow

blooms. Among the white trumpet daffodils, Scapa lasts extremely well when cut. Orange Bride, with beautifully frilled tangerine crowns, is well worth considering, too. Bulbs should be planted in the garden in the autumn for flowering in March and April.

DAHLIAS

One of the most vivid and colourful of garden flowers, the dahlia is a half-hardy plant. (The tuberous root has to be lifted before the winter and returned to the garden in the late spring). Originally from Mexico, it was brought to this country in the sixteenth century. As distinct from the single-flower type, the cactus dahlia is becoming more and more popular. (You can see lovely examples of these blooms in the colour photographs facing page 65.) They can withstand heavy

Above, a formal arrangement of daffodils, where both buds and fully opened blooms have been used. Below, daffodil buds and blooms in a line design, with young rhubarb leaves hiding the pinholder and a stone from the sea-shore placed to keep the flowers well apart

Right, spiky cactus dahlias are grouped together in a bowl-shaped container to form a charming arrangement. Long sprays of ivy leaves provide a graceful outline

rain and rough winds. Of course, all dahlias need attention, with regular watering, plenty of humus in the soil and disinfecting against fungus. Seed can be sown at the beginning of April, or cuttings can be inserted into pots of sandy soil any time from February to the end of April. They flower from August to October.

FREESIA

Grown from bulbs, these flowers with their delicious scent and beautiful colours can bloom either in bowls in the house or outside in the garden. The shades of freesia blooms vary from pure white to carmine, through delicate shades of pink, rose and lilac, as you can see from our photographs facing page 56. Plant them in the autumn for flowering in the spring.

FUCHSIA

This is a very attractive plant, with an unusual pendant shape and rich mauve and purple colours. In the garden it can be trained into neat bushes or into small standard trees. A perennial, once established it needs little attention and will keep coming up year after year. A cut stem or two will add a note of graceful interest to your smaller mass floral arrangements.

GERANIUMS

A dense and vividly-coloured flower, the geranium is an annual, and can be grown inside and outside the house. The roots do, however, need drying in the winter before replanting in the spring. With its bright reds, pinks and white petals, the geranium is ideal for plant arrangements or for low mass designs.

GLADIOLI

Another of our older garden flowers, gladioli lend themselves wonderfully to any flower ar-

rangement. Easy to grow, the corms are planted in the spring and the plants will flower in the following September or October. Among the yellow and white gladioli, Leif Erikson has many flowers on a spike open at the same time. In the pure whites, White Herald and Andes are among the earliest to bloom. Richard Crooks has creamy white petals flushed with pink and a throat of deeper red while among the deeper reds, Tobruk does not grow too tall and its blooms will stand wet weather without spoiling. In the large-flower variety, the deep mauve Mable Violet and the purple tinged Viola are particularly impressive.

HOLLYHOCK

Yet another really old English flower – it was introduced in 1573. It's actually a perennial but because it gives a much better performance when young is often treated as a biennial. Single hollyhocks are the taller and more enduring plants. But all types like a rich, not too light loam with plenty of manure – seeds should be planted in May for flowering in August.

HYACINTHS

These may be grown from bulbs either indoors in bowls or outside in the garden.

With their delicate fragrance and pretty colours, hyacinths can be aranged in many attractive designs. See our photograph facing page 64 for an example. In the open, they like a rich, light soil and can be planted from September to the middle of November. For indoor flowering, the bulbs should be planted about the end of October.

IRISES

Originally from Spain and Holland, the purple "flag" iris makes a brave, gay showing in gardens everywhere throughout the month of June while the paler, bluer Dutch iris comes out in May. Irises range in colour from blue to yellow, white,

Above: A few Shasta Daisies taken straight from the garden may not seem very interesting, but with a little care and ingenuity a charming effect like the one above can be achieved. The stems have been cut to various lengths and some tall ornamental grasses added. Below, in a lovely arrangement, the first early spikes of gladioli are combined with a little of their own dark foliage in a pewter jug set on a matching tray

red and brown – and there are exotic varieties which combine colours, for instance the Lady Mohr which is a mixture of ivory, brown and chartreuse. Lovely in line designs, they can also be used most effectively in mass and many other floral arrangements.

LUPINS

These lovely tall spires of colour can be planted either in April or in October. During the last ten years some hundred colour combinations have been developed, including yellow and crimson, and red and orange. The lupin is, of course, ideal for line designs, but several stems can look charming in the more informal mass arrangement of garden flowers.

MARGUERITES

Another bloom that is attractive in mass designs, the marguerite actually belongs to the Chrysanthemum family, but does, of course, need far less attention. It will succeed in almost any soil and the large, daisy-like blooms appear throughout the greater part of the year.

MONTBRETIA

These slender, arching plants appear in many gardens, and their red, yellow or orange flowers can make a bright splash of colour in your floral arrangements. The slim green leaves are also very useful for background purposes.

PANSIES

A charming little flower, which is especially suitable for miniature arrangements in decorative containers, such as silver mugs, bon-bon dishes or small wicker baskets. Years ago pansies were known as "heartsease" but the blooms were smaller and there was a more limited range of colour. Nowadays we can choose from flowers of one pure colour, or from charming and picturesque mixtures. There are two seasons for planting – autumn and spring. When very early spring flowers are wanted, plant in autumn, say in early October. When planting in spring, chose early

consider these lilies

Often associated with luxury and extravagance, in actual fact lilies can be economical, for they last a long time when cut and are easy to grow in the garden or in bowls indoors. All lilies need plenty of water and it helps to make them last longer if you add half a cup of vinegar to each two quarts of water you use for the arrangement and when topping up. While lilies can be effectively used in various kinds of vases, their regal qualities seem emphasised when arranged in glass. Above, arum lilies have been arranged in a design which shows to the best advantage their purity of colour and elegant shape. Right, two Gold-Rayed lilies of Japan have been inserted into a glass scent bottle and held in position with foliage. Below right, sprays of lily-of-the-valley have been arranged with their leaves folded over in a fan shape in a shell vase

A simple but charming arrangement using only one kind of flower – six irises in bud with their stems cut at different lengths and inserted into a shell container (hold them firmly with Oasis). The buds open slowly, and will bring fresh colour into your home every day for a week. Buds, incidentally, are always easier to arrange to good advantage than fully formed blooms

March so that the pansies will be well established before the really warm, sonny weather arrives in April and May.

PRIMROSES

Often growing wild, these fresh little flowers make delightful spring bouquets and designs. They bloom as early as January in the warmer parts of the country, but are probably at their most profuse and best in March.

ROSES

The traditional flower of England, and one of the loveliest and oldest. Of course, there are almost endless varieties nowadays, from the wild Dog Rose with its pale pink petals blooming in the hedges, to the long-stemmed, elegant Floribundas. With their lovely range of colour and texture, roses are a flower arranger's delight—you can use them in almost every conceivable way, line, mass, informal, low cluster—the possibilities are immense. Garden-wise, it is also a most satisfactory plant. The well-known rose grower Harry Wheatcroft has often said that all that is needed is a "good heart and a bucket of muck". They can be planted from the end of October to the end of March. Pruning should be done either in early March or in December-January. There are various basic types of roses. Hybrid Tea Roses, for instance, are the bush type of two to four feet that flower in June and July and again in September. The flower itself usually has a rich perfume and an elegant bulb-shaped centre. There is an extensive colour range. The Floribunda type has developed from the polyanthus and so the flowers are generally in attractive clusters. They are very hardy and constantly in flower. The Rambler type have small flowers which appear in showy clusters during June or July while the Climbers, lovely against a wall, come in shades from scarlet and copper to pink and yellow. The miniature roses – six to twelve inches high – come from Spain and Holland.

SCABIOSA

Another perennial, this is sometimes known as the pincushion flower. It starts to bloom in late June,

PICK OF THE SEASONS

Autumn in all its splendour is represented by this arrangement of mixed bold-faced dahlias in a blue china soup tureen. Turn flowerheads in and out, using natural stalk twists to give variety to the outline. Arranged by Irene Hazell, F.R.H.S.

A festive display for Christmas has been achieved here with five white chrysanthemums, a few glass balls, ivy foliage, holly and a large silver star. The design was built up in a goblet vase on a pin holder, the star being set in place first, and then the tallest flower inserted

CHRISTMAS DESIGNS

Right: one spray of white chrysanthemums arranged on a flat dish around a central candlestick. Some artificial fern and holly, a few gold-painted flower-heads, pine cones with coloured glass balls all make up a display that is both artistic and right for the season

A celebration centrepiece, below, made of pink rosebuds and carnations combined with foliage, bows and gold balls. The design is arranged in a partly open basket in damp Oasis. The candlestick on the right is necessary to give height and balance to the arrangement

Winter, *when flowers are scarce and expensive, is the time for improvisation. White chrys-*
anthemums last for days (as each separate outside petal turns brown it can be removed
gently without spoiling the flower) and they harmonise well with honeysuckle berries

with blue, purple or white petals, and continues flowering for some months. It is best planted in March or April.

STOCKS

A popular garden flower, with delightful colours and sweet fragrance, stocks are extremely easy to grow. Seeds can be sown from February to May and will flower the following year in June, July and August. Colours vary from pink, purple and mauve to white and crimson and all in-between shades. In our photograph facing page 33, you can see a beautiful arrangement where stocks and thistle leaves have been used to create a most striking effect.

SWEET PEAS

These charming, butterfly-shaped flowers begin to bloom in late June and are at their best in early July. They can be arranged in so many ways and whether in a mixed bunch or on their own, provide a lovely clear pool of colour. There's a beautiful example facing page 48. Every year sweet pea breeders submit the best of their new varieties to the trials at Wisley, so that there are always new and improved varieties coming along. One recent award which will provide a cool and fragrant bowl for home decoration is Blue Vein. Fireglo provides a startling scarlet while Milky Way is a deep cream with contrasting blush pink at the petal edges.

TULIPS

Lovely for formal designs, there are so many varieties and shades of tulips nowadays to bring spring into your home. Tulip bulbs should be planted in October and November for flowering in April and May. When arranging tulips, remember that the leaves can be made to look extra graceful by gently twisting them round a finger. The petals can be gently bent over to make larger looking flowers for special effects. Don't worry if the stems are not absolutely straight – curved stems can be most attractive in an arrangement. If, however, you prefer straighter stems, see the chapter headed, "How to make cut flowers last" which begins on page 107.

A dramatic line arrangement in many rich shades of Red Hot Poker or Kniphofia. The long snake-like stalks will twist and turn in an upward movement if they are arranged in a flat dish. A little laurel foliage which has been treated with glycerine will not only hide the heavy pinholder which holds the stalks steady but will provide a central point for the whole arrangement

Roses are an ideal flower for arranging on their own — shades, texture and shapes all so perfect. Here are two examples to show you just how lovely roses can be. Above, cream roses arranged in a flat glass dish. The tallest bud was inserted first, and then shorter buds to form the outline. More mature blooms made up the centre. Below, the same basic design was followed, but Floribunda roses in trailing sprays were used for a higher and more full arrangement

FLOWERS ON SHOW

In the beginning, when your interest in the art of flower arranging has only just started, the suggestion that the day might come when you will exhibit your designs at a Flower Show may seem beyond belief. However, as you progress, encouraged by the admiration of others and your own increasing confidence, you will find yourself examining more and more closely the flowers displayed in Shows. Eventually you may feel that the time has come for you to enter something of your own.

You may already belong to a Flower Club or a Horticultural Society whose regular shows include flower arrangements. Or you may decide to exhibit your work at one of the garden parties or fêtes arranged by various organisations – political groups, charity committees, churches, schools, Women's Institutes Townswomen's Guilds – during the summer.

Most Flower Show organisers include in their schedules a class for beginners, one that is easy and uncomplicated. This is where to begin. Valuable experience is gained by exhibiting in even a small way and can lead to greater things.

So, having decided or been persuaded to enter a Show, how to go about it? First of all, read the schedule carefully. If there are items you do not understand, write to the Show secretary at once and make sure that you are clear as to what is needed. Only those who compose the schedule can give the answer; don't depend on the opinion of your nearest and dearest!

Decide next which class you will enter; and on the basic style and shape of your design. Bear in mind the points on which it will be judged: originality, design, freshness of flowers, colour scheme and suitability of container – and do your best to fulfil them.

Having decided on your arrangement, practise it as often as you like, so that it becomes easy and so there is no chance of unforseen snags –

like the beautiful display of flowers that fell over just as the judge came along because its holder was inadequate.

In plenty of time, collect together all the equipment you will need for the arrangement (together with a few extras in case of accidents). These may include pin holders, wire netting, wire, plasticine, flower scissors, a bucket for water, a long-spouted watering can and, of course, the necessary containers and accessories, to which should be added on the day of the Show the flower and plant material.

Your flowers and foliage should be chosen carefully and looked after well. Carry the material to the hall carefully packed into a box or if possible in a bucket with a little water. On arrival fill the bucket with water to allow for a long, deep drink.

These hints will be found useful:

1. Pick flowers and leaves late at night or early in the morning.
2. Pick most flowers in bud, recutting their stems under water and leaving them in deep water. They can be moved from light to dark and warm to cool places to aid or retard their opening.
3. Split stem ends of woody plant material before placing in the vase.
4. Submerge all leafy shrubs in water overnight. Split stem ends.
5. Foliage should be dusted and all damaged leaves removed.
6. Submerge in water for at least two hours, more if possible, most flat surfaced leaves, including begonia rex.
7. Some glossy leaves, such as camellia and laurel, can be wiped with an oily rag but do not allow any oil to show.
8. Branches can be trimmed to shape, obvious cuts disguised with water colour paints or rubbed with another branch.

FLOWERS

Here and on the following pages are designs which will inspire you whether you are a beginner or are already up to exhibition standard. All of

Left: Mrs. Cole of Kenton, Middx., won a first prize at the National Association of Flower Arranging Societies Competition with this basket. Copper beech sprays gave necessary height and motion and she added red-purple Jackmanii clematis and some brilliant red Baccarat roses. Below: Mrs. Harry Dean's arrangement for Christmas won a second prize. She used tree prunings, skeletonised leaves, fir cones, holly and ivy and completed it with candles, berries and bells. Finally she sprayed with glitter dust

ON SHOW

them were Show entries, most were also prize winners, but their value lies in enchanting variety of style and in ingenious use of the materials chosen

Right: using bulrushes and white Colvilleii gladiolus in a water-side arrangement, Mrs. A. G. Thorne was awarded the first prize in the class headed as "Tranquility" at the Festival of Flower Decoration. Below: Mr. V. R. Vynes Brooks of Southport won a first prize at the National Rose Show with this lovely basket of blooms. Arranged with their own foliage, the roses are all in different shades of pink — the varieties are Madame Butterfly, Coral, Pink Garnet. Roses rarely need additional foliage

Left: Mrs. F. Lamb won a first prize for her collage of flowers, foliage, fruit and tall candles which was also voted "Best in Show". Below, left: this basket of flowers was arranged by Mrs. Frank Hopkins for the class "To carry to a friend". Below: Three broad funkia leaves provide a foil to the tall, spiky iris spears in this flowerless display which was entered by Mrs. H. W. Hall of Lymington, Hants. and won a second prize

Right: this rhythmic design in a candle-cup holder held by a white china model won a first prize for Mrs. Perrin of London. Almond blossom was used to form the fine Hogarth curves of the outline while magnolia blooms in graduated sizes provided the main interest. Glowsy green leaves gave a contrast in texture and the background was draped with a fall of pale blue net

Left: a pottery bowl of mixed miniature flowers arranged in moss won a third prize in its class for exhibitor Mrs. Parker. This is an "all round" arrangement, one which looks attractive from all angles. A round container is the obvious choice in this case

Above: an original design by Mrs. N. Farrish is based on a curving and lichened branch of pine representing a tree, and a piece of wood representing a mossy bank in winter. Two little birds sit snugly in their nest with their Christmas stockings hanging by their sides and wait hopefully for Santa Claus! Left: "Green grow the Rushes-O" – Mrs. Doris Hickson of Thames Ditton, Surrey, was awarded first prize for her arrangement of bulrushes, grasses and foliage in a shallow container. She used two model flamingoes for balance

UNUSUAL CONTAINERS

There are undreamed-of treasures hidden in your house. Here, metal jelly moulds have been polished up and transported from the kitchen to the drawing room to grace spring daffodils. Look around your own home – almost anything with a pleasant shape, however shallow, that holds water can be used as a container

UNUSUAL
CONTAINERS

Large ornamental shells are once again popular – this time for floral arrangements. Get out Granny's old Victorian shells and wash them in warm soapy water, insert some Oasis and arrange your flowers in a design like this lovely one by well-known Julia Clements

A large, spiky shell makes an ideal vase for sweet peas. Mrs. Amy Cooke, whose hobby is flower arranging, followed the gentle line of the shell with her blooms. She used Florapak to hold them in place and gave them a thorough, gentle watering every other day

Above: the attractive Chinese tea-pot is echoed in Mr. G. H. Pitt's entry, "China Famille Verte". The shallow round bowl contains a branch, stones and blooms

Below, left: for her delicate, and charming interpretation of the class "Flowers and china" Mrs. Denham-Davies of Hookwood won a well-deserved first prize

Below: Miss Ena Collis's design seems to suggest spring's new awakening. Catkins combine with daffodils, narcissi and hyacinths to shelter the little china deer

Above, left: Mrs. K. Perkins of Mill Hill, London, won a first prize for her arrangement of colourful fuchsias. Note the triangular shape of the display.

Above: this delightful line design was made by Mrs. P. D. Woodman of Southgate, London, and was awarded the second prize. Beech leaves, gladioli and pom-pom dahlias are mounted on a flat board.

Left: a bowl of miniature mixed flowers was the exhibit of Mrs. A. B. Lane of Moreton-in-the-Marsh, Gloucestershire

Above: rushes, foliage and dried husks arranged into a shapely triangle won a first prize for Mrs. Elizabeth Kay.

Above, right: elegant triangle of arum lilies and leaves built round a slender statuette by Mrs. A. Gotobed of Hounslow was awarded a first prize.

Right: for Christmas this tableau arranged on a satin drape has as its focus three hellebores – Christmas roses. The tall candles add height. This arrangement, also by Mrs. Gotobed, won a third prize

ARTIFICIAL FLOWERS ... AND PLANTS

During the long dreary winter months we all feel a need for colour and freshness in our homes – and just when flowers are at their most expensive! Too often we forget the fresh appeal of growing plants, and that artificial flowers and foliage have never looked more natural

Almost incredible improvements have been made in plastic flowers; nowadays we are often hard put to it to tell whether the flowers in a vase are real or artificial. And it is even possible to buy perfumed plastic flowers!

The advantages are obvious – they last for years, need no attention once arranged and bring a touch of colour to your room. You can see from the photographs in this section just how easily they lend themselves to attractive arrangements.

The stems can be bent into graceful curves, the flower heads can be twisted to turn exactly the way you want them to go and the base of the stems can be folded to the right length. Use plasticine or modelling clay in the bottom of the container – poke the stalks in firmly and no other aid to positioning will be necessary.

Some very lovely and striking arrangements can be made by using plastic flowers with fresh foliage or small branches. It is often possible to obtain slender branches of pussy willow months before the traditional burgeoning at Easter and these combine effectively – and lastingly – with many plastic flowers. Lilac branches, stripped of their old brown leaves and kept in water, will often grow little green buds and these too can be used effectively. Don't forget to add a little water to the container whenever you use fresh foliage.

Plastic flowers may collect a little dust especially in a centrally heated atmosphere. They can be quickly freshened by a gentle wash in warm soapy suds. Rinse away the soap and, after a gentle shake, leave them to dry away from direct heat.

Plastic flowers may seem expensive at first sight, but when you consider how they will last and last – to say nothing of the pleasure they can give – they are enormously economical.

Plants are another ideal way of making the most of winter. The day has gone when single plants were placed in china or plastic pots and left to stand in isolated glory – nowadays we have realised that there is an art in grouping plants just as much as there is in arranging flowers.

The grouping of plants as a decoration appeals to every arranger both for the satisfaction it gives and for the beauty of the collective effort. So never be afraid to repot your plants – grouping three or more in a larger, more attractive container. When choosing plants for an arrangement, look for height, depth and focal interest, just as you would with a flower arrangement.

One of the joys of plant arrangements is that, once sturdily established, they do not demand unending attention. Many people find the attraction in making groupings is in testing their ability to combine certain shapes and colours in the vast variety of containers that can be brought into use.

Plants such as sansevieria, grevillia and croton are excellent for establishing height in a grouping, while the large-leafed begonia rex, dieffenbachia and ficus will give depth. Smaller plants with variegated colourings such as peperomia maranta

This beautiful arrangement is composed entirely of plastic flowers and foliage. The white shaggy chrysanthemums provide the focal interest. Available bloom by bloom or as an arrangement from John Lewis, London

and chlorophytum will add focal interest, and any trailing plants such as ivy and tradescantia are excellent for side placements.

Perhaps the best advice to give any would-be indoor plant arranger is not to be too ambitious at first. Many people are deterred from keeping indoor plants because they have met with one or two failures; but it is quite possible to be successful by starting off with a few easy-to-grow plants, leaving the more difficult ones until you have become more practised. Ask your florist's or nurseryman's advice.

Many plants in their native home enjoy cool shade; others like a moist, warm but not sunny atmosphere, so in general it is important to keep indoor plants away from direct sunlight and from draughts. But although draughts are not liked,

ventiliation is, so do not be afraid to open the windows so that the plants can get oxygen.

Avoid sudden changes of temperature – that is, a hot room in day time and a cold room at night. See that the day and night temperatures do not vary more than 10 °F.

Fork over the top soil now and again to aerate the earth, and remove all dead or yellowing leaves.

In spring and summer feed your plants fortnightly from a miniature bottle of fertilizer, following the manufacturer's instructions. Keep the soil moist; how often to water it will come by experience. Less water, and no food, should be given in winter, the plant's resting time.

Be careful to water only from the bottom the plants with fleshy leaves, such as African violets and begonia rex. Stand them in a saucer and

Left, a delightful arrangement all in fresh green and white with the flowers, leaves and berries all in plastic. It is available from Dickins & Jones and the arrangement, with vase, costs approx. 4gns. On the right you can see a Poinsettia, a traditional Christmas-time indoor plant. The leaves at the top of the plant are a cheerful red, becoming variegated lower down, and at the base are an attractively veined dark green. Plant by courtesy of Monro Ltd, Covent Garden

allow the roots to take up the food or moisture. Do not allow water to fall on the leaves. Hot water in the saucer will often give the necessary humidity needed by the plant.

As plants vary so much in their requirements, it is better to buy a plant for a particular room, bearing in mind the exact position in which it will eventually stand.

Picking the tips off trailing plants will make the main plant more bushy and you can repot after three years.

Plants that are excellent for decorative groupings are: *begonia rex*, which has red, silver, purple, and green leaves. Water from the bottom and keep away from direct sunlight. *Chlorophytum* has thin, spiky green and white striped leaves, and is very easy to grow but it is best kept

out of direct sunlight. *Cissus Antarctica* – or the Kangaroo Vine – is a tall climber and does not need much water. *Fatshedera lizei* grows fairly well and has leaves like very large ivy. *Fatsia Japonica* has large deep-lobed green leaves which fall at all angles and is fast-growing. It likes a cool shady spot. *Maranta* comes in several varieties but the kerchoveana, with emerald leaves with brown velvety spots, is especially effective for the base of a grouping. It likes a warm, moist atmosphere. *Tradescantia*, or Wandering Jew, comes in green and white, and purple and green. A trailer, it is good for wall brackets. The tips can be pinched off and will root easily in soil or water. *Asplenium nidus* – Bird's nest fern – is a glossy green plant, very easy to grow, with long, leathery leaves with wavy edges.

Sometimes your indoor pot plants can be improved by some judicious pruning of leaves, plantlets or little tips. These small prunings should not be discarded, often they will blend beautifully in an arrangement of flowers and provide focal interest. On the left, a charming foliage arrangement composed of a few leaves of lily, hosta, bergenia, pelargonium, canna, gesneria, curtonus and maple

Left, yet another example of a pretty arrangement of mixed foliage, this time in a round pottery bowl. The leaves include begonia rex, fittonia, iris, holly, fern and euonymus radicans. Note how the display has height at the back for balance and depth and how depth and sharp focal interest come from the variegated leaves

*Artificial flowers have never been lovelier. Choose and display them with care and the fav-
ourite flowers of spring and summer will bloom in your home all year round. And they're ideal
for centrally heated rooms. Here, golden daffodils mingle with lily-of-the-valley and mimosa*

Plants, as well as flowers, need the arranger's hand

Don't be afraid to re-pot plants, combining them into distinctive group effects. Here, cissus antarctica gives height to an arrangement of hydrangeas and azaleas. with various foliage providing interest to the display

Below, African Violets. Here, instead of buying one big pot plant, several small ones are grouped together in a shallow bowl. Note the charm of the subtle contrast of the pink and blue

Above – a miniature sea garden arrangement, using cactus and sea-shells, by Julia Clements. Sea coral was fixed to a tray base with Plasticine, and then backed with a potted cactus so that the container was hidden. The tray was filled with sand and studded with small shells, and small plants such as alysum were added. Below – the definite, severe lines of cactii are contrasted with the delicate flower-patterned pots which are both distinctive and appealing

Artificial flowers, cleverly arranged, can be as attractive as a display of natural blooms. Here, scarlet and creamy-tinted carnations combine with sprays of fern to make a lovely arrangement. Note how the burnished copper of the vase adds to the effect

This beautiful triangular arrangement of dried flowers and grasses in a stemmed wine glass will last throughout the winter and beyond. Available, from Dickins and Jones

DRIED FLOWERS

Another way of having flowers in your home through the winter is to make a shapely dried arrangement.

Clear-cut designs and contrast in shape and texture of material are essential for success but the subject is endless and absorbing.

Dried flowers and grasses may be bought from florists and department stores, often dyed in bright colours – although the natural shades are preferred by many flower arrangers. One of the most fascinating of all sidelines of flower arranging, however, is that of drying, pressing and preserving flowers and leaves at home.

There are four methods of preserving material and after a little experimenting you will quickly become accustomed to using the one that best suits your purpose.

The upside-down method

This is used for flowers such as delphiniums, larkspur, astilbes, golden rod, celosia, helichrysum, achillea, love-lies-bleeding and many others. They should be picked just before maturity and hung upside-down in small bunches in a dark dry cupboard or attic, preferably where air circulates. The dry atmosphere will absorb moisture and the darkness will prevent the colours from fading.

The borax method

This treatment is suitable for more open flowers, such as pansies, Canterbury bells, zinnias, marguerites, daffodils, etc., for with this way the form as well as the colour of the flower can be preserved.

Cover the bottom of a deep box with powdered

Above: a quietly charming arrangement with an eastern effect created by the Oriental statuette, water and stones. Iceland poppy buds, sorrel, a few sprays of oats and some spiraea have been used

Below: dried flowers also combine with fresh ones, an economical as well as an attractive proposition! In this flowing arrangement in a low bowl, dried thistles blend with dark red roses and driftwood

borax. Strip off all leaves from the flowers and shorten the stems, then stand them on the borax and continue to sprinkle it round, under and over the flowers until they are completely covered. Leave for about three weeks. The powder should then be poured off very carefully.

The glycerine method

This is used for most types of foliage; branches of leaves placed in the solution will keep indefinitely. Wash the leaves to remove dust and split the ends of the stems or branches. Place the material in a jar containing 1 part glycerine to two parts water, enough to reach about four inches up the stem. Leave for two or three weeks in an airy place. Beech leaves should be picked late in August or early in September.

The pressing method

Ferns and other flat-surfaced leaves can be preserved by pressing between newspaper and some very interesting lines and shapes can be retained. Funkia leaves can be folded double and placed between sheets of newspaper; iris, gladioli and raspberry leaves can be dried in the same way. Plenty of newspaper should be used to absorb the moisture and heavy books placed on top.

Pussy willow and bulrushes dry well out of water and interesting shapes can be obtained with broom if you wrap it in newspaper and bend it to the desired shape, leaving it to dry in position.

Skeletonising

The Victorian hobby of skeletonising leaves has come back into fashion and these can give a delightfully ethereal touch to a dry arrangement. Magnolia, iris and galax leaves respond well to treatment. Boil the leaves for thirty minutes in a quart of water to which a teaspoon of soda has been added. After leaving to cool in the water, spread the leaves out on paper and with the back of a knife scrape off all the fleshy parts, taking care not to tear the leaves. Place in some bleach water and leave for an hour, then rinse in clear water.

Finally, wipe the leaves carefully with a soft cloth, press between sheets of blotting paper or newspaper, weigh down and leave overnight.

HOW TO MAKE CUT FLOWERS LAST

Flowers that look so lovely in the garden are sadly short-lived once they are cut for the house. And bought from the florist their lives seem even shorter. But once you know how, there are all sorts of little tricks which will keep them looking happy around the house for many more days.

Ideally, if flowers are to last and keep their brightness and colour for the longest possible time, their stems must absorb water easily. There must be no air lock between the water in the container and the stem; and bacteria, which blocks the stems and keeps the water out, should be discouraged from developing.

There are a number of preparations on the market which can be added to water to prolong the life of cut flowers but in many cases a simple household commodity – such as sugar or aspirin – can be used instead to keep flowers fresher for longer. For more detailed information and the requirements of individual flowers, look at the chart beginning overleaf.

If you have a garden, choose your blooms and cut them very early in the morning or at dusk, when the flowers are at their freshest. Never gather them when the sun is beating down. Flowers are ready for cutting just before they are fully in bloom: roses should be in tight bud; gladioli with the first flowers just opening; sweet peas before the top flower is fully open. Lupins are best picked when only the three lowest rings of flowerets are open.

Immediately after cutting, place the flowers into deep water in a bucket and stand this in a cool, dark place for several hours before arranging. (For the few varieties which do not require this first long drink, see the chart.) Remove the leaves from the stems.

Leaves tend to take in a great deal of water

which then transpires (or evaporates) from their comparatively large flat surfaces at a much greater rate than from flower heads. In this way leaves will deprive their own flower heads of water if leaves and bloom are left on the same stem.

Most large-surfaced leaves and leafy twigs will remain stiff and strong if submerged in water and left overnight before use.

Flowers with hollow stems, like delphiniums for instance, are often particularly difficult to keep looking fresh. Placing the base of the stems into boiling water before arranging them in the vase can help to keep them at their best for longer. Delphiniums (and lupins too) will also benefit from having their hollow stems filled with water after cutting, then plugged with cotton wool before being left overnight in deep water to be conditioned.

Hollow stems should be cut straight across, not on a slant as with other flowers, before being filled with water. The best way to do this is with a medicine dropper or a meat baster – the type which has a rubber bulb on the end of a short tube, available from household stores. Fill the stem slowly and with care in order to avoid causing air bubbles and so stopping the water from reaching the flower head.

The stem base of flowers with milky sap, such as poppies, for instance, should be dipped into boiling water or held over a naked flame for a minute. When cutting blooms like these it is useful to have near you a jar of fine sand so that you can immediately dip the stem into it to seal the cut and prevent loss of sap.

Cut all stems, with the exception of the hollow ones, on a slant so that they rest lightly on the bottom of the vase. Carnation stalks should be cut between notches. Flowers with woody stems, such as roses, lilac, rhododendrons, viburnum and others, should have the base of their stems crushed before they are put into water so that they are able to drink deeply. Cut flowers from the florist should be recut an inch or so from the base of the stem and then, as with garden flowers, put into deep water in a cool, dark place for several hours.

Cut away the white portion of the stem ends of flowers grown from bulbs as they drink only from the green portion. Hold the stem ends of daffodils, narcissi, etc., under warm running water to remove the sticky substance that is extuded. Tulips will always twist and turn towards the light. If this happens and spoils your arrangement, try wrapping them up to their heads in newspaper and leaving them overnight in deep water. Next morning they will be stiff and straight again.

Fleshy-stemmed flowers should have an inch or so cut from their stems under water before being left for their first long drink. They are cut under water in order to prevent that choking air bubble from forming.

Because it is so important, something worth repeating is the necessity of making sure always, before starting any arrangement, that the vase or container you plan to use is scrupulously clean. It is good practice to give each one a scrub directly after discarding a faded arrangement – never, in fact, to put away an unwashed vase. Remember, too, to rinse your pin holders under running water regularly.

Always have some water in the vase before starting to make an arrangement in order to prevent the stem ends from becoming dry. For mixed displays like our lovely arrangement on the previous page, add two tablespoons of sugar to a quart of water, or a tablet of charcoal, to keep the water pure.

The water in which your flowers are to be arranged should have the chill off. Afterwards, a daily topping up with fresh tepid water is all that is necessary. Emptying vases daily and refilling them is needless and can be positively harmful. Flowers do not like excessive handling. If with some particularly long-lasting flowers (sweet peas, chrysanthemums, etc.) you find that the water has become sour after four or five days or so, take the vase to the sink and run fresh water into it, letting the water spill over the top of the vase until it runs freshly once more.

Flowers grown from bulbs – tulips, daffodils, narcissi and so on – flourish with two or three inches of water in their containers.

The chart which follows gives instructions in detail for individual types of flowers and their treatment – both before and after being arranged. In every case the treatment is simple but well worth the time and effort involved.

HOW TO
MAKE
CUT FLOWERS
LAST

FLOWER	PREPARATION	ADD TO VASE
ANEMONES	Cut stems on slant. Submerge to heads 1 to 2 hours until texture of flowers is firm	¼ cup vinegar to 2 cups water
APPLE BLOSSOM	Can be picked in bud. Crush stem base, allowing it to drink more water quickly. Blossom can be sprayed with hair lacquer to prevent petals falling	2 tablespoons ammonia to 2 quarts water
AQUILEGIA	Put stems into boiling water for exactly 20 seconds to discolour stems slightly	5 drops peppermint to 1 pint water
ASTERS	Place stems in boiling water for 1 minute	2 tablespoons sugar to 1 quart water
BEGONIAS	Pick and arrange	2 tablespoons salt to 2 quarts water
CANTERBURY BELLS	Place stems in boiling water for 45 seconds only	2 tablespoons washing soda to 2 quarts water
CARNATIONS	Pick when fully open. Cut stems on slant between notches with sharp knife	Cold water only
CHERRY BLOSSOM	Place stems in boiling water 1 to 2 minutes. Smash stem with hammer	Cold water only
CHRYSAN-THEMUMS	Crush stems. Place in bolling water 2-3 minutes, then cold water	10 drops oil of cloves to 2 quarts water
CLEMATIS	Pick and arrange	2 tablespoons medical alcohol to 1 pint water
COSMOS	Pick when centre is smooth, before pollen ripens	1 teaspoon sugar to 1 pint water
DAFFODILS	Cut above white stem base, place in 1 in. very cold water, leave in cool place ½ hour, arrange in 1 or 2 in. of water	Cold water only
DAHLIAS	Place in 2 to 3 in. boiling water 1 minute, then immediately into cold water. When in vase, change water daily	5 tablespoons medical alcohol to 2 quarts water
DELPHINIUMS	Cut stem under water. Place in boiling water 1 minute, then into cold water. OR fill stem with water, plug with cotton wool	2 teaspoons sugar to 1 pint water
DIANTHUS	Submerge to heads for 1 hour	1 tablespoon alcohol to 1 pint water

FLOWER	PREPARATION	ADD TO VASE
EVERGREEN LEAVES	See method for leaves, below	1 tablespoon glycerine to 1 quart water
FERN (Maiden Hair)	Never pick until seed pods on back of leaves are brown. Sear ends over flame. Submerge in cold water 12 hours	Cold water only
FOXGLOVE	Place in boiling water for 30 seconds	Cold water only
GAILLARDIAS	Place stems in boiling water 1 minute	Two tablespoons salt to 1 pint water
GERBERAS	Pick when open a few days. Place in boiling water for no more than 1 minute	Cold water only
GLADIOLI	Pick when first flowerets are open	Five tablespoons vinegar to 1 quart water
GRASSES	Dip stems in vinegar	Cold water only
HELLEBORES (Winter and Lenten Roses)	Split stems and place in warm water or submerge ½ hour	Cold water only
HYDRANGEA	Pick well-developed, firm heads. Remove most leaves. Crush or scrape stem, place in boiling water 1 minute	Cold water only
IRIS	Pick when just opening. Cut above white stem base under water. Dip in boiling water 1 minute, place in deep water	Three drops peppermint to 1 quart water
LARKSPUR	Pick when first flowers are open Place in boiling water 1 minute	Cold water only
LEAVES Beech Magnolia etc.)	Submerge overnight and leaves will be firm and stronger. Condy's crystals in water will brighten colour	Preserve in 1 part glycerine to 2 parts water for 3 weeks
LILACS	Remove young side growths with sharp downward pull except for leaf near head. Split and crush stem, place in fairly warm water until ready for use	Cold water only
LILIES	Cut stems on slant to prevent curling	Half cup vinegar to 2 quarts water
LILY OF THE VALLEY	Change water frequently. Keep cool. Wrap stems in wet face tissue, even when arranged	¼ cup vinegar to 1 pint water
MARGUERITES	Pick when centres are smooth, before pollen ripens	1 tablespoon salt to 1 quart water
MARIGOLDS	Place in boiling water one minute	1 tablespoon sugar to 1 pint water
MIGNONETTE	Remove lower leaves. Burn ends, never boil. Place in deep warm water	1 tablespoon salt to 1 pint water
MOCK ORANGE	Remove all leaves. Crush or scrape stem	Cold water only

FLOWER	PREPARATION	ADD TO VASE
PEONIES	Place in boiling water 30 seconds only	3 tablespoons sugar to 1 quart water
POINSETTIAS	Scrape well and boil ends one minute	1 handful rock salt to 2 quarts water
POPPIES	Pick when bud is erect or at sunrise when just opening. Boil ends one minute. Plunge in deep water	Cold water only
PRIMROSES	Dip stems in boiling water 30 seconds to seal	Cold water only
RANUNCULI	Pick when centre is smooth before pollen ripens. Boil ends 30 seconds. Place in cold water.	Cold water only
ROSES	Cut stem diagonally with sharp knife and scrape ½ in. of stem. Dip in boiling water 1 to 2 minutes and arrange in warm water. The warm water travels faster, acting as a stimulus to the flower. If arranging in a silver vase, place 1 or 2 copper coins in base; this offsets the detrimental effect of silver on roses	2 tablespoons salt to 1 quart water
SCABIOUS	Pick when one circle of flowers or petals is open. It will finish opening in water and last longer	Cold water only
SCHIZANTHUS	Pick when about 8 flowers are open	Cold water only
SNAPDRAGON	Cut stems diagonally with a sharp knife. Never store with other flowers, as snapdragons give off a gas which kills all other blooms	2 tablespoons salt to 2 quarts warm water
SPIREA	Shake to dislodge loose petals Smash stem ends with hammer	Cold water only
STATICE	Pick when fully open	3 tablespoons sugar to 1 quart water
STOCKS	Remove most foliage. Crush or scrape stems, then place in boiling water 2 to 3 minutes	1 tablespoon salt to 1 pint water
SWEET PEAS	Plunge in hot, them cold, water	2 teaspoons sugar to 1 pint water
TIGER LILIES	Remove most of foliage. Scrape stem for 2 to 5 in.	Cold water only
TULIPS	Cut above white base of stem. Roll individual blooms completely in wet newspaper an hour or two to keep stems straight	Cold water only
VERBENA	Pick when one circle of flowers or petals is open. It will finish opening in water and last longer	Cold water only
VIOLAS	Pick when fully open. Submerge 2 hours in iced water	¼ teaspoon salt to a small vase of water
VIOLETS	As for violas	As for violas
VIBURNUM (Snowball)	As for hydrangea	As for hydrangea
ZINNIAS	Place stems in boiling water 1 minute, then plunge in cold water	Cold water only

LOCATIONS

In designing an arrangement, one of the first questions to ask yourself should be, "Where is it going to stand?" The answer to this question will help you to decide on the colour of your flowers, on the shape of your vase and even the style of your arrangement.

If you live in a modern house or flat, decorated perhaps in white and red, and wish to spend a day in the country searching for material, you should carry in your mind not only the colour scheme of your room but its size and shape and exactly where your arrangement will finally be placed in this room.

You might look for red berries to be preserved later and arrange them with bare branches. Green leaves would surround the red berries to add boldness. Black elderberries would look equally well if arranged with foliage in a white vase but you would pass by the brown sprays of dried dock, Queen Anne's lace, ivy and grasses, which would be ideal in an arrangement designed for a room decorated in autumnal shades of brown, orange, green.

Of course, there are times when it is only possible to make the best of what is available but even so the answer to, "Where will it stand?" will settle a number of your doubts as to how to begin.

If you wish to fill a corner in a small room which allows no space for a mass display, try a tall vertical design placing the accent on the vase.

All designs for low tables should be made so that you can look down on them and also into them. No focal points are required but attention should be paid to colour harmony.

Mantel-pieces need careful thought. Line designs have a special place here if the shelf is low and narrow, whilst a modified, tall mass design would suit a wider one. A triangular design is excellent if the flowers are to be the centre-piece, whilst a diagonal line should be introduced if the arrangement is to stand at one end of the shelf.

Mass displays look beautiful in large rooms and equally so on a hall table, providing a bright welcome to guests as they arrive.

Flower arranging for the table depends very much on the setting and on the occasion for which the flowers are required. As a general plan, try to keep them low so that they are neither easily tipped over nor difficult to talk across when people are sitting down.

One idea is to design your table arrangement to echo one of the main colours in the room – the curtains, perhaps, or a dominant picture. Or try the effect of a one-colour scheme set on a contrasting table cloth. The relationship of the flowers to the cloth or mats, china and glass is most important, so keep the entire setting in mind all the time.

The finishing touches to your arrangement are best made in place so that you may have a good, overall look at it.

This holds true whatever style or shape of arrangement you have made, and for whichever location it is intended. You will see it against its background, which can change the original appearance out of all recognition.

Certain problem spots of your home can also be helped by careful use of flowers. For instance, a dark hall can be improved by an arrangement of large, light-coloured flowers, preferably in a mass style to provide an immediate point of impact and to dispel any illusion of gloom. In the same way, flowers can make a dark alcove seem lighter.

Flowers and windowsills seem natural partners and so they are – but bear in mind these few points. An arrangement can be spoiled if light

Right, geraniums and cow parsley in a shallow bowl. Start with tallest flower (1); arrange in tight dome. Fill in with foliage, add geranium leaves, starting with the centre and then working outwards to each end of the dish

Below, echo shine of metal cigarette box by using shiny-leaved flowers – marguerites, daisies or marigolds. Start with tallest flowers (1,2), then group shortest (3, 4, 5) at far end. Fill in with medium sized blooms

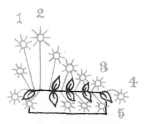

The satin richness of an old, polished copper jug makes a perfect foil for the freshness of country flowers. Here freesia and stocks were used with ivy leaves. Insert tallest centre bloom (1) first. Then arrange shorter flowers around it like spokes of a wheel (2-5). Fill in the outline more solidly with remaining flowers and foliage

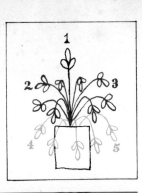

shines in through the stems. To avoid this, build up a cluster of blooms (rhododendrons, perhaps, stripped of their leaves and displayed in a medium high, wide-necked vase). Do not leave flowers standing in front of a window in full sunlight or you will find that they will wilt much quicker than you expected.

In the same way, do not forget that frost can strike through glass and condemn your flowers to death by leaving them on the windowsill at night when temperatures are likely to drop sharply. And don't leave them standing over a warm radiator, either!

Arrangements in wall vases are attractive and especially useful if you have few available surfaces for standing displays. Since wall arrangements are usually fixed at eye-level or higher, the longest stem should be cut to exactly one-and-a-half times the greatest dimension of its container; no more or the effect will be over-elongated.

When designing an arrangement for a wall container, think in curves – look for shapely stems and make use of your skill in curving suitable material yourself. Wall containers are not usually suitable for pin holders. Wire netting should be used instead to hold the material although in certain cases Oasis will be adequate.

Floor-level arrangements in the home usually apply to the fireplace. This, the focus of so many sitting-rooms in this country, is an eye-catching position and in summer when the fire is not required a lovely flower arrangement also serves the purpose of hiding the empty grate.

As with arrangements on low tables, fireplace displays will be looked from above so in this case make your main stem much taller than usual – two or two-and-a-half times the height of the container is a general guide. Apart from that, stick to the usual basic principles of balance and composition, placing the larger blooms in the centre of the arrangement; leave spikier flowers and foliage to make the outline.

Above: this summer display would be an ideal arrangement for a side-table or wide mantelpiece. It consists of peonies, delphiniums, sweet peas, roses, penstemon and begonia leaves. Below: a formal design of leaves and flowers, this would be marvellous in an alcove or as a bright spot in a dark hall. The roses are dark but the rest of the material is all very light

TO STAND

Table flowers will be viewed from all sides and this should be kept in mind when planning a design for table decoration. As you build up the arrangement place the flowers so that they turn in and out to all directions and yet present a smart profile to all corners of the room. Above: a simple display of spring flowers in a polished copper bowl illustrates perfectly an attractive all-round arrangement of flowers which is to stand in the centre of the table, which itself stands in the centre of the dining room. The flowers used are daffodils, irises, anemones, lily of the valley, ivy. Left: another spring arrangement, this time a triangular design which will be viewed mostly from the front but because the back will also be seen care has been taken to show depth and focus behind as in the front. The flowers include irises, tulips, narcissi, gladioli and mimosa

ON THE TABLE

Above: this is an example of the "three-way" arrangement; two other "faces" are made by placing another large leaf centrally and low at the back and building smaller focal points on either side of it so that the deep goblet container may be turned and the arrangement will show an interesting variation of balance, depth and focus. The flowers and foliage include roses, martagon lilies, salvia, spiraea, with a few begonia rex and iris leaves.
Above, right: an arrangement in a low basket is ideal for any table since it is built as an "all round" design and is also easily moved whenever necessary. In bright and summery array the flowers include oriental poppies, kniphofias (red hot pokers), delphiniums and foxgloves.
Right: this charmingly exotic and delicate arrangement of white roses with syringa, clematis and branches of lime is in an antique china bowl

ARRANGED AGAINST A WALL

This is where mass styles come into their own, for a plain background enhances the flowers magnificently. Left: summer's bounty, a glorious arrangement of flowers in all shades of pink and orange with green and grey foliage for good effect. Roses, geraniums, peonies, stocks, are mixed in with sprays of trailing escallonia, hosta and begonia rex

Below: a curving design has been built up in a punnet on Oasis. Roses and chrysanthemums combine with berries and a few leaves

Above: this asymmetrical triangle has been built in a foil-lined silver cigarette box. Long and pointed iris leaves make the outline which is then filled in with iris blooms, delphiniums, cornflowers, poppies and some broad hosta leaves

Right: a large and lovely array of mauve and white lilac has been combined with a few carnations and some auriculas. The whole beautiful arrangement has been set in a classical urn

On a windowsill, *far left, flowers will smell even better and look even more eye-catching. Here, roses and lilies in pink, white and gold are in elegant array with blue hydrangea heads*

On a tray *made from an old mirror, above, flowers will be seen in reflection as well. Tall irises, gaillardia, kniphofias, foxgloves and one or two dark carnations are in a circular arrangement*

When using blossom, *a tall vase allows a natural fall. Here mauve flags were used with laburnum. Crumpled wire mesh is held in place at the top of the vase by Sellotape. Sprays at the base echo the main design in a small, separate container*

For a low table, *above, a delightful arrangement of Japanese quince blossom has been enhanced by placing it in the unusual oriental dish. The branches are held by a hidden pinholder*

On the mantelpiece *right, the stone contrasts with the freshness of this spring bouquet. See, too, how the darker foliage against the plain wall focuses attention on the fully-opened daffodils*

For a dark corner

Transform those awkward, dark pla-
ces – a corner of a room or perhaps
an odd niche in a hall or on a lan-
ding – into a place of real beauty by
a flower arrangement like this. By
using lilies in a dual vase, this lovely
triangle design brings a wonderful eff-
ect of light and space to a dim corner

A pinholder is essential for this kind of arrangement – here it stands in aluminium foil, well hidden by a pretty begonia leaf

HOLDERS AND EQUIPMENT

If you wish to arrange your flowers in your own home in an expert fashion then you will need a certain amount of equipment. It is all comparatively inexpensive and could be acquired over a period of time. But as you progress to more and more adventurous or expert arrangements, so you will find the need for certain equipment, such as holders and wire mesh, becomes more imperative.

All the things mentioned here should be obtainable at florist's or department stores.

To start with, wire netting is an item you cannot be without. You should buy a yard of this (two-inch mesh is a good all-round size) and cut it in pieces that will completely fill your vases when crumpled. Keep a piece for each individual vase, as after one or two uses the wire netting will take on the shape of the container. Generally used in conjunction with a pinholder, there are times however, when wire netting should be used on its own – a container with a very narrow bottom, a very deep vase or a tiny one such as a wineglass or very shallow bowl. You can counteract the wire's tendency to rust by always adding a pinch of borax to the water in the vase – this will not hurt the flowers in any way. Mesh is an absolute essential for any arrangement with flowers set horizontally just above the vase's rim.

Pinholders come in various shapes and sizes, and are invaluable for holding flower stalks securely. Some of the heavier pinholders are strong enough to support heavy branches. They are used by themselves, without wire, for Japanese flower arrangements, but always make sure that the actual pins are covered by water. The base is generally of a lead alloy, with pins of brass, but there are plastic based holders now on the market which are slightly less apt to rust. But again, a pinch of borax in the water will help.

In nearly every case, the pinholder will need to be firmly fixed to the inside of the container. This can be done with modelling clay or with Plasticine. If you should at any time be caught without either, remember that a surprisingly firm cement can be made from Tide. Just mix about a cupful of the powder to a stiff paste with about two tablespoonsful of water. It will take about an hour to set firmly.

This detergent cement is also useful in many other ways; for you can use it for any dried arrangement – just pile the mixture into the vase

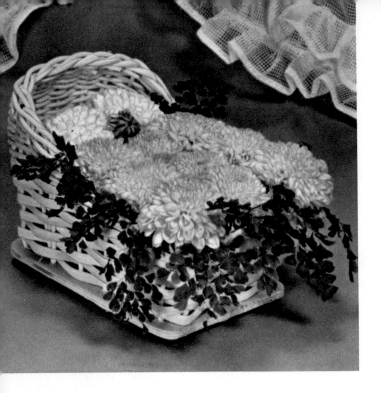

The arrangement above would make a charming little gift for a new mother. Inside the cradle-shaped basket was filled in with Oasis which had been saturated in water, and short-stemmed flowers and leafy twiglets were then pushed into the Oasis. Below: to make the most of this design for spring flowers, the tankard was filled with crumpled chicken wire. The stems of the flowers could then be slotted through the mesh at any angle desired

and go ahead with your arrangement. A good pull will be enough to remove the cones or seedheads later and the "cement" will dissolve if immersed in warm water.

When using Plasticine, make sure that both of your hands, the plasticine and the container are dry; otherwise you may have difficulty in making it stick firmly.

The old-fashioned glass holders that were once commonly used in rose bowls are now made in plastic and unbreakable materials. They are good for an all-round upward display, but leave little scope for making really artistic arrangements.

A useful piece of equipment for supporting long, heavy branches in tall vases is a piece of tin shaped to fit round the stems and bent so that it will hang on the inside of the rim.

Cages, which are exactly what their name describes, are very useful and especially so when used in shallow, very open containers. They take the place of the crumpled, sometimes clumsy-appearing, wire netting and will fit neatly over a pinholder.

Candlecups, almost like an extra container, are essential for narrow-necked vases or very small or slender containers. Shaped almost like a champagne glass but in a gilt or silvered light metal, they need a little touch of adhesive material – Tide, Plasticine or modelling clay – around the base and then they can be inserted into a hollow, either in the neck of the vase or even in a figurine. If you are interested in line or oriental arrangements, you will find candlecups invaluable for they can be used on a low base and easily concealed with a piece of wood or a stone.

It is well worth while, incidentally, making a collection of any attractive pieces of wood and stones or pretty pebbles. They will come in useful in so many of your arrangements. Whenever you are at the seaside, keep a look out for driftwood – it often can be found in unusual and interesting shapes – and for smooth, coloured pebbles as well as for shells of all kinds. And, of course, a country walk can be an ideal chance for collecting attractively shaped small logs of wood and stones, which can all be used over and over again, both to conceal the mechanics of your designs or to add interest.

Oasis is a dark-green spongy substance which,

The picture above shows some of the equipment which the flower arranger will find most useful. Key is as follows: 1, metal base for container. 2, wine bottle for use as vase. 3, florist's tube for adding height. 4, seashell container. 5, popular pottery container. 6, a metal base on which to stand an arrangement. 7, candle-cup. 8, plasticine. 9, flower scissors. 10, three different pin-holders, including one "well" type which is its own container. 11, wire netting. 12, clamp for holding driftwood. 13, block of Oasis, one of several sizes

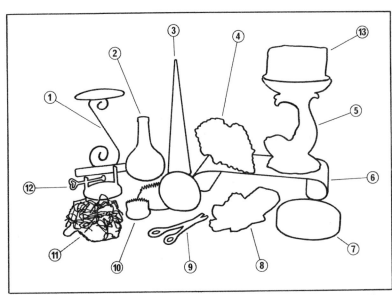

123

Cage

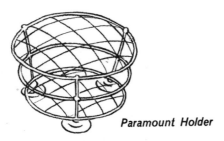

Paramount Holder

Cages, made in three sizes so that they will fit over most pinholders, take the place of wire mesh. The Paramount holders, with a suction pad at the base, can be used instead of, or with, pinholders. Below, wire netting used in two differently shaped vases

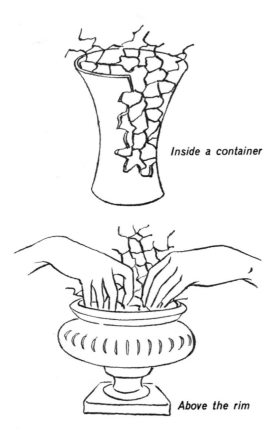

Inside a container

Above the rim

placed at the bottom of your container and water poured into it, will hold flower stems securely. It can be broken into little blocks or pressed into the shape of your vase. It holds moisture well and can be used two or three times and costs from 10d. a block. Florapak costs from 2s. 6d., and is somewhat similar but is best dampened and then crunched up until it is pliable enough to fit into the container. It does tend to break up into tiny pieces and work its way into the stems of flowers, so on the whole Florapak is best kept for single occasions – a special arrangement for a party or a dinner-table, for instance. Being white, Florapak is ideal in a transparent glass container. Naturally, both Oasis and Florapak can be used very satisfactorily in glass or very precious or fragile containers as they will not scratch the sides.

Raffia is always useful, and especially for low, full arrangements in an unusually shaped container. It can be used to tie the stems of your flowers together in little bunches, which can then be "planted" separately into the container.

Lemonade straws are useful, too. Inserted into hollow stems, they can lengthen stalks which are too short for a particular arrangement. The water is sucked up through the straw just as if it were a natural stem.

Do keep a pair of scissors especially for use with flowers. The best kind have a serrated edge which helps to crush the fibres in the stems and so make it easier for the blooms to absorb plenty of water. It is also a good idea to keep one or two deep buckets only for flowers. If you have a garden, instead of the more usual trug for cut flowers the ideal thing is to collect the flowers in a plastic bucket partly filled with water. As each flower is cut, put it in the bucket, so that any chances of wilting are immediately reduced.

Of course, it would be wonderful if we all had a separate scullery with stone floor and sink where all flower-arranging could be done—but for most of us that is something of the past. We can, however, take a tip from the Victorians and keep all our floral arranging equipment together. Wherever you keep it – perhaps in a large box, or in a drawer – you will find it an enormous help if everything you are likely to need is always kept clean and tidy in the same place.

Above, sprays of variously coloured chrysanthemums are securely held in a triangular design by a pinholder concealed by leaves and set upon a wooden breadboard

In the dignified arrangement below of irises and pyrethrums, a "well" type pinholder has been used effectively instead of the more usual kind of container

Above, a little piece of Oasis inserted into the mouth of a polished sea-shell and well moistened with water acts as a firm holder for carnations, blooms and leaves

WINTER FLOWERS
AND BERRIES

Those lucky enough to have their own gardens always have plenty of flowers for the greater part of the year, but during the late autumn and winter months there is sometimes a shortage of material for cutting. Indeed, from the floral arranger's point of view, the time from towards the end of October to March can be very frustrating, when there is so little in the garden that will lend itself to colourful designs. So here is a list of the plants and shrubs which are most useful for this purpose. By careful choice, it should be possible to incorporate new plants into the garden so that there will be enough colourful blooms and leaves to fill the vases throughout the long, dark months. Don't forget, too, the decorative effect of leafy sprays, berries and even well-shaped small bare branches. Some very lovely effects can be achieved from what may seem at first rather unpromising material.

HARDY FLOWERS FOR CUTTING DURING THE WINTER MONTHS

NAME	COLOUR	PERIOD
Chrysanthemums	various shades	October and November
Nerine Bowdeni	pink	October
Amarcrinum Howardii	pink	October
Schizostylis coccinea	red	October and November
Schizostylis Mrs. Hegarty	pink	October and November
Viburnum bodnantense	white-tinged pink	October to March
Viburnum fragrans	white-tinged pink	October to March
Roses	various shades	October and November
Rhododendron Nobleanum	red	November to February
Rhododendron Nobleanum album	white	November to February
Prunus subhirtella autumnalis	white-tinged pink	November to March
Erica darleyensis	pink	November to March
Jasminum nudiflorum	yellow	December to March
Helleborus niger	white	December and January
Garrya elliptica	green	December and January
Arbutus unedo	white	December to February
Chimonanthus fragrans	pale yellow	December to March
Helleborus corsicus	pale green	December to March
Hamamelis mollis	golden yellow	January and February

NAME	COLOUR	PERIOD
Cyclamen europaeum	rosy crimson	October
Cyclamen neapolitanum	pink	October
Iris unguicularis	blue	December to March
Snowdrops	white	January and February
Cyclamen Coum	rosy crimson	January and February
Erica carnea	various shades	February and March
Abeliophyllum distichum	white	February and March
Camellia J. C. Williams	pink	February and March
Camellia oleifera	white	February and March
Camellia Sasanqua	rose pink	January to March
Amygdalus communis	pink	February and March
Amygdalus communis Pollardii	rose pink	February and March
Amygdalus Davidiana alba	white	February and March
Forsythia Giraldiana	yellow	February
Forsythia ovata	yellow	February and March
Rhododendron Moupinense	white	February
Rhododendron mucronulatum	rose purple	February
Berberis Japonica	yellow	February
Rhododendron scabrifolium	pink	February
Rhododendron dauricum	rose purple	February
Rhododendron lutescens	yellow	February and March
Rhododendron Ririei	purple	February and March
Rhododendron Stewartianum	various	February and March
Rhododendron barbatum	brilliant red	February and March
Rhododendron Seta	pink	March
Rhododendron Cilpinense	pink	March
Rhododendron praecox	rose purple	March
Leucojum vernum	white-tipped green	March
Pieris floribunda	white	March
Pieris japonica	white	March
Camellia japonica	various colours	March
Corylopsis pauciflora	pale yellow	March
Cydonia lagenaria	red	March
Forsythia intermedia spectabilis	yellow	March
Anemone appenina	blue	March
Anemone fulgens	scarlet	March
Erica arborea alpina	white	March
Ribes sanguinea splendens	red	March
Prunus Conradinae	pale pink	March
Prunus yedoensis	white-tinged pink	March
Prunus cerasifera Blireiana	bright rose	March
Corylopsis spicata	yellow	March

SHRUBS WITH BERRIES SUITABLE FOR CUTTING DURING THE WINTER MONTHS

NAME	COLOUR OF FRUITS	PERIOD
Callicarpa Giraldiana	violet	October and November
Clerodendron trichotomum	dark blue	October and November
Euonymus europaeus	pink	October and November
Euonymus europaeus fructo albo	white	October and November
Euonymus latifolius	red	October and November
Euonymus oxyphyllus	blood red	October and November
Euonymus planipes	rosy red	October and November
Berberis Jamesiana	bright red	October and November
Berberis aggregata Prattii	brilliant red	October to December
Berberis rubrostilla	coral red	October and November
Berberis subcauliata	coral pink	October and November
Cotoneaster bullata	brilliant red	October to December
Cotoneaster Dielsiana	scarlet	October to December
Viburnum lanatum	red	October to December
Viburnum betulifolium	red	October to December
Hippophae rhamnoides	orange	October to January
Cotoneaster pannosa	dark red	October to March
Cotoneaster conspicua	brilliant red	October to March
Cotoneaster rotundifolia	red	October to February
Cotoneaster Harroviana	bright red	October to March
Hymenanthera angustifolia	white	October to January
Viburnum Henryi	red	October to January
Viburnum lobophyllum	red	October to January
Pernettya mucronata	crimson	October to March
Pernettya mucronata alba	white	October to March
Pyracantha angustifolia	orange yellow	October to February
Symphoricarpus racemosus laevigatus	white	October to February
Pyracantha Gibbsii	red	October to January
Pyracantha Rogersiana	orange	October to January
Ryracantha Rogersiana flava	yellow	October to January
Stranvesia Davidiana	red	October to March
Stranvesia undulata	red	October to March
Skimmia Fortunei	red	October to March
Skimmia japonica	brilliant red	October to March
Pyracantha Gibbsii aurea	yellow	October to January